how to start a home-based

Personal Chef Business

HOME-BASED BUSINESS SERIES

how to start a home-based

Personal Chef Business

Second Edition

Denise Vivaldo

Guilford, Connecticut

Text design by Sheryl P. Kober

ISSN: 1931-3101
ISBN: 978-0-7627-6366-5

Printed in the United States of America
10 9 8 7 6 5 4 3 2 1

Contents

Introduction

The personal chef business remains a fairly new phenomenon in America, but one that is growing and thriving. Hiring a personal chef is no longer only for the rich and famous, but for people in every economic level. It's as common in some cities as paying a neighborhood teenager to mow your lawn. The key to success in the business is understanding the market where you live and customizing your service to fulfill your community's needs.

Twenty-five years ago I was a personal chef, even though the title hadn't been invented yet. I was a chef-for-hire, working for several different families. I cooked in their homes and left them their meals. It was a wonderful way to start my own business, create a client list, and grow into catering. I was simply a new chef, trying to find a career in food without having to work in a restaurant.

I hadn't thought of that time until I was invited to speak at a personal chefs' conference. It was there that I found out my catering book was one of the personal-chef industry reference books that new personal chefs were using to figure out the business end of their cooking careers. Even with the courses available, they still needed to know more about how to price their menus, how to charge for their services, and how to create other income streams. I met many new cooking colleagues, and we stayed in touch over the years. Some of them answered questions and made great recommendations that I used in this book.

These days, I spend my time food styling, writing books (my latest being *The Food Stylist's Handbook*), teaching, and speaking. I'm still active in the United States Personal Chef Association (USPCA) and enjoyed being a keynote speaker at the 2010 conference in Denver. Some of my favorite people in the world are personal chefs. Personal chefs are natural nurturers; they want to feed you and make you feel better. What's not to love?

One of the trends I see emerging in the personal chef industry is the use of social media as a major marketing tool. Having a blog, a Facebook business page, and a Twitter account are the new business cards. It's an ingenious strategy because it gives the chef the power to present himself and his cuisine exactly how he wants to be presented. It can be personal, it can be silly, or it can be conservative and strictly professional. It's also super cheap; for very little overhead, you can put yourself out there and make a huge impression. The sky's the limit!

Another trend I see is personal chefs adapting their services to meet each client's needs. Gone are the days of the 5x4 (five meals, four servings each). Well, not that it's gone, but I see more and more chefs offering shop- and prep-only service, or dinners only, or a once-monthly service where they freeze almost everything. The more we can be flexible in our thinking, and innovative in our approach to different clients, the more people we can make happy (not to mention more money in our bank accounts).

This book is a very good starting point for personal chefs. It will point you in the right direction, helping you find the path to a long and fulfilling cooking career. Networking organizations and personal chef groups that you may want to join, for information as well as moral support, are listed in appendix E. I'd advise each reader to take the time to find out which group is the best fit for you. I find that most people involved in food are naturally generous. It's a constant gift to increase your network. Every person you meet can help you. And in turn, try to help others when you've had success. My career has been shaped by generous mentors. Particularly, I am very grateful to Gail Kenagy of the USPCA.

Speaking of thank-yous, I've found that my friends, family, and colleagues have helped me every step of the way. Whether it was a loan, a pat on the back, or a few words of inspiration, other people have been a great help to me.

My business is a big part of my life. I wake up each day grateful for the chance to cook great food, make money, and have fun . . . all at the same time. In the twenty-six years of striving and thriving, I've had several women that worked with me every step of the way. I couldn't have done it without them.

Since 2001, Cindie Flannigan has worked with me at my food styling company, Food Fanatics. She arrived as an intern from my alma mater, the California Culinary Academy in San Francisco. She never left. No matter what food project we are working on, Cindie is there to research, help, support, edit, and generally make it better. And, on top of all that, we get to laugh a lot. It's because of Cindie that this book got written. It's easier to sell a book than it is to write it. You're going to have to trust me on that one. Newer to my world is Mandy Unruh, who has taken over all my social media and has kept me hip and up-to-date. She's also a personal chef in her own right and is invaluable to me in keeping current with the personal chef marketplace.

Please stay in touch with us at www.foodfanatics.net and www.foodfanaticsunwashed.com, and tell us your success stories. We can't wait to hear from you!

Best regards,
Denise Vivaldo

So You're Interested in Becoming a Personal Chef

You've looked at your life and career choices and have decided to try your hand being a personal chef. But, being a cautious person, you want to find out more about this exciting field. Personal cheffing is a great job for independent and self-motivated people who love to cook, want to be their own boss, and have control over the hours they work. This book will tell you what it takes to succeed.

The personal chef (PC) field has grown by leaps and bounds over the last twenty years and shows no sign of slowing down. David McKay and Susan Titcomb, original founders of the United States Personal Chef Association, said that the perception is that it is a service for the rich, much like having a maid service was back in the 1970s. The first maid service was established in 1974, and the first maid franchise in 1979. Today there are more than 35,000 housecleaning services across the United States. The personal chef business is still in its infancy, with the current economic environment and people's increasingly busy lives contributing to the increase in demand for personal chef services. More people today feel they have less time to cook for themselves but still want high-quality, healthful food. As more people realize they can hire PC services for less than it costs to order out or buy takeout every week, more and more people will start seeking out qualified personal chefs.

Many consumers today consider opening up a box or a can to be cooking. Even more people say they don't know how to cook and have no interest in learning. A big part of the reason is that as children, they didn't see anyone cooking at home, so they grow into adulthood without any culinary instincts or skills.

The single most important element in being a personal chef or running a successful personal chef business is the food. Make quality food and make it consistently. Clients will hire you because they don't want to stress about their meals. Every time they eat one of your meals, they should say, "*This* is why I hired a personal chef."

Another thing to remember: Your clients are inviting you into their homes, often when they are not there. They eat the food you prepare for them. In order to hire you, they have to trust you. You need to realize that this is of the utmost importance. Trust is a two-way street. If you care about your clients, you will ensure long-term success.

Whether they run a cafe, teach cooking classes, or operate a catering business, I have never met a successful chef that does *not* have a genuine need to feed people.

Personal Chef: A Definition

A personal chef is someone who provides meal planning and preparation for individuals or families on a regular basis. A personal chef prepares meals according to clients' culinary preferences and dietary requirements. Personal chefs shop for groceries and prepare meals in their clients' homes.

After establishing a client's meal requirements, the personal chef plans on an agreed number of menus tailored to the client's needs and subject to the client's approval. The job includes buying the food, cooking the meals, packaging the meals with heating instructions and refrigerating or freezing them, and cleaning up afterward. Generally, a personal chef will cook once a week or every other week for each client, preparing enough food for four to six meals at a time. The typical service is known as a 5x4 service, which consists of five entrees of four servings each. This is a total of twenty individual meals for that client.

Personal chefs are *professionals* and present themselves as consistently neat and clean, thus inspiring confidence. T-shirts, caps, aprons, and chef's jackets (cleaned, pressed, and in good condition) are all appropriate, and personalizing these garments with a business name or logo is a great way to advertise your services. You will meet potential clients in every store you shop in. Make a great first impression.

Personal chefs don't expect their clients to have any special equipment or ingredients, but clients' kitchens should have the following basic appliances in working order:

- Refrigerator
- Freezer
- Oven
- Stove
- Countertops cleared for your work space
- Microwave
- Sink with hot running water

Unless you're cooking for your mom, every personal chef should have all other cooking supplies as part of his or her own portable kitchen. This will include any small electric appliances you might need, cutting boards, all ingredients needed for that day, pots and pans, mixing bowls, utensils, and disposables.

If you are thinking about catering as an eventual career, starting as a personal chef will give you experience and confidence that will be invaluable later on. When you have some cooking experience under your belt, you might want to try apprenticing with a local caterer as the next step. This is a great way to gain exposure and experience and to improve your production skills.

The Traits of a Good Personal Chef

A passion for cooking is an essential element for being a personal chef. But is it enough? Starting, running, and maintaining a business requires characteristics that have little to do with creativity or culinary skills. An honest appraisal of your own strengths and work-style preferences will help you determine whether becoming a personal chef is really a good choice for you.

One good example of this is to consider whether you like working alone. Working in a restaurant or catering kitchen offers lots of camaraderie and a fast pace with set schedules, a boss, colleagues, and deadlines to keep everyone on track. Being a personal chef is a solitary occupation, though sometimes a client is at home and may expect pleasant small talk. There's no one but you to keep you on schedule and help you manage your time.

The checklist on the next page will help you think through whether you'd enjoy and excel at being a personal chef.

If you answer yes to more than twelve of these questions, then being a personal chef may be right for you.

Y	N	
❏	❏	Do you love to cook?
❏	❏	Do you make excellent meals even when you're not feeling your best?
❏	❏	Do you have a strong working knowledge of food preparation and menu planning? (If you don't understand this question, the answer is "no.")
❏	❏	Do you have a basic understanding of nutrition and the new FDA food pyramid?
❏	❏	Is your home kitchen well organized?
❏	❏	Do you keep your work area clean and tidy when you cook?
❏	❏	Do you have a strong working knowledge of food safety and sanitation?
❏	❏	If you are missing an ingredient in a recipe, are you able to improvise and still get delicious results?
❏	❏	Are you happy when you work alone?
❏	❏	Are you confident and resourceful?
❏	❏	Can you cook without recipes?
❏	❏	Can you cook dishes that you don't personally like?
❏	❏	Do you enjoy all types of food?
❏	❏	Can you stay polite and unruffled when people are picky, change their minds often, or have no idea what they really want?
❏	❏	If you budget $50 for a particular shopping trip, are you able to stay within that amount?
❏	❏	Have you had good results selling products and/or services before?
❏	❏	Will you be comfortable selling yourself in this new career?
❏	❏	Is there a market for personal chef services in your area? (Find this out as soon as possible. And ask yourself; if not, why?)

Who Hires a Personal Chef?

People who hire a personal chef usually do not have the time or ability to cook for themselves but have the resources to hire someone else to do it for them. Some people are too busy because of their work schedule or family obligations. Others may just want to free up time so they can do things they enjoy more than cooking. Some people might be tired of restaurant or take-out food, and some may not know how to cook and have no desire to learn.

I was executive chef of a large catering company when one of my clients approached me about becoming his private chef. He offered me too much money to refuse, and as I was looking for a way to cut down on my hours so that I could write my book, *How to Start a Home-Based Catering Business*, I accepted his offer. After a few weeks at my new job, I realized that I could get all my work done in two days, had time for my writing, and still had time left over. I introduced myself to neighbors and told them about my services, and before long I was fully booked. Suddenly I was a personal chef! In those days it was called a chef for hire.

There are increasing numbers of people who want to improve their health or want help with special diets. Many managed weight-reduction programs are very expensive, and hiring a personal chef can be less than the program itself.

Some people have special medical considerations that may include specific food allergies, high blood pressure, high cholesterol, or fat- or calorie-restricted diets. As personal chef Cathy Marella-Luce points out, clients with special diets are "pretty overwhelmed with their dietary restrictions. There is no one to guide them and certainly few people to make these new, total lifestyle changes taste great. That's where a personal chef's creativity and knowledge about spices, flavors, etc. really can bloom and make their new restricted diet not feel so boring and bland."

Many consumers today are adopting organic, vegetarian, or semivegetarian diets. There are many reasons people choose particular diets. They may feel that grazing

Vegetarians Defined

Vegetarians eat no meat, although they may eat fish, eggs, or dairy.

Vegans are strict vegetarians who consume no animal products. This includes eggs, milk products, and honey.

Ovo-lacto vegetarians do not eat meat but may consume animal products like eggs and milk products.

Lacto vegetarians do not eat meat or eggs, but may consume milk and milk products.

Ovo vegetarians eat eggs but do not eat milk products or meat.

I talked to personal chefs across the country to ask them about their experiences and have scattered their information and advice throughout the book. A list of the personal chefs who helped me appears in appendix D.

Who Decides to Become a Personal Chef?

Personal chefs come from wildly varied backgrounds, but I think they all have two things in common: They are passionate about food, and they want to make a difference in the lives of others.

Laura Cotton, a PC since 1999, previously had a job that didn't allow her time for a social life. Now that she cooks for a living—something she has enjoyed since she was a child—she has time to volunteer in her community.

Jeff Parker was looking for an income he could live on without having to work for someone else. Brian Ramirez, who's been working in the field for nearly a decade, says that the regular week was a huge plus for him compared with the weekends and holidays he'd have to work as a caterer.

Cathy Marella-Luce was miserable in her job as a technology strategist and wanted a career that made her feel she was contributing to the world in some way. Connie Breeden didn't want the long hours that catering and restaurant work required, causing her to miss too many holidays and family events.

Hoyt and Lydia Eells, a couple who have been PCing for the last ten years, were looking to channel their love of food into something that would supplement their retirement income. John Bauhs says that PCing offers a "life-long skill development opportunity . . . always great things to learn . . . it offers cerebral and physical challenges, and it fulfills my desire to help others create better and healthier lives."

Another reason people choose this career is it allows those who are parents to spend more time with their children. Scott Wilson wanted to be home in time to meet his then-eight-year-old daughter at the bus stop. Pauline Reep had her own catering business, but that took her away from her three small children too often.

cattle destroy potential farmland. Or their objection to eating meat can be an ethical, political, or even religious one. Ask potential clients why they chose their particular diet. You can make better decisions on their menus if you understand their motivation.

The Importance of a Culinary Background

Do you have to go to cooking school? The short answer: No. The long answer: If you have strong production skills (and you only get strong production skills by going to cooking school or working in a restaurant or *both*), you will produce more meals in less time, and this equals profit. You can't make money if you move slowly or are inefficient. You only learn speed and efficiency with practice. Lots and lots of practice. On my first day of culinary school, I grilled pork chops for 300 people. I'd love to tell you I did a great job, that my chops were moist and had perfect grill marks, but I'd be lying. By the time I graduated, I'd learned the order and conformity of a grill system. It involves method, timing, and movement. If I hadn't had the opportunity to grill pork chops over and over and over again, I would have taken forever to get it.

Culinary schools provide rigorous, hands-on training and give students the opportunity to perfect cooking methods and skills that it would take years to acquire otherwise. Home cooks may not know how to plan their time to cook a week of meals in one day or that *brunoise* is the French culinary term for a 1/8-inch cube knife cut, but they can easily learn. What is most valuable is an intuition about food, what tastes good with what, how to make substitutions, and how to cook three dishes at once.

Another thing that you will learn at a cooking school and probably nowhere else is safety and sanitation. You have no idea how important this subject is until you've taken the class. Ignorance on this subject is *not* bliss—and it can be deadly. Attending a course on the subject is the best way to learn (contact the National Restaurant Association for ServSafe classes in your area), but if you simply are not going to take a class and nothing said here will convince you, then *please* read one of the following books on food safety:

- *ServSafe Essentials*, 5th Edition, (Prentice Hall, 2010).
- *Essentials of Food Safety and Sanitation*, David McSwane et al (Prentice Hall, 2004).
- *Quick Reference to Food Safety and Sanitation*, Nancy Rue and Anna Graf Williams (Prentice Hall, 2002).

The desire to learn is very common among culinary professionals. Whether you choose to attend a culinary school is up to you and your checkbook, but there are many classes offered to help you be successful. Continuing education classes, short or long cooking school programs, and classes in restaurants or private homes are all excellent places to learn more about food. The USPCA (United States Personal Chef Association) and the APCA (American Personal Chef Association) offer classes to their members that provide valuable, targeted information for personal chefs. You can get more information about these and other personal chef associations in appendix E.

It is important to keep in mind that you are representing an industry, and your clients are going to judge that industry based on their experience with *you*. The more you know, the better you will present yourself and, in turn, the industry. All classes you take will add to your knowledge and confidence, making your skills more valuable and marketable, and eventually will create more profit for you. The more confident you are as a chef, the easier it is for you to charge for your services.

Different Clients, Different Food

You will have many different clients who all have different ideas about food. If you think that because you make the best lasagna in your family you can succeed as a personal chef, you will be sorely disappointed, and so will your customers.

The key to a thriving personal chef business is learning as much as you can about food. It's a process that never stops. If you are fascinated with food, you will constantly learn new things. If food isn't your passion, you will not learn and you will not grow.

I've learned new things about food and cooking from every situation I've been in. I've learned from travel and from teaching, from food styling and from food writing. What I'm trying to say is that you will need a broad culinary experience to draw from because not everybody wants to eat the dishes in which you specialize. Experience can be gotten in a variety of ways. And if food is your thing, what a joy the research can be!

Some clients may specifically request that you cook with their pots, pans, knives, and cutting boards. For an example, if your client wants to keep kosher, you cannot use cookware that has been used to cook non kosher foods. Kosher food conforms to strict Jewish biblical laws having to do with the type of food that may be eaten and to the kinds of food that can be combined at one meal. Pork and shellfish are not kosher. Combining meat and dairy products is not kosher. Animals that are consumed must be killed and cleaned according to Jewish law. Utensils that have come into contact with meat may not be used with dairy, and vice versa. Utensils that have come into contact with non kosher food may not be used with kosher food. Again, talk with your clients and be sure you understand all the rules. Or call a local kosher caterer or restaurant and ask them if you can study with them for a weekend or during the holidays when they are very busy and you can be a needed extra pair of hands.

Cooking for the Convalescing

One group of people who could use your services are the people who cannot cook for themselves, people who are disabled or recovering from an illness or surgery. Eating a healthy diet is especially important during this time. Fresh fruits and vegetables are often requested parts of a recovery diet. Appetite is usually lower than normal, so it's a good idea to provide smaller, more numerous meals to encourage food intake.

It is important to discuss what types of food your client likes and to work that in with what is recommended by their doctor when possible.

A serious injury or illness can have enormous emotional impact. This is especially true for those with chronic medical problems. Having a sense of humor, being patient, and allowing extra time for your client to talk (you may be the only person he or she sees that day) will not cost you anything and will greatly help his or her emotional state. I learned early in life that it doesn't cost anything to be nice.

Whatever the reason your clients hire you, discuss their particular needs with them so that the service they expect is the service you provide.

What You Need to Know about Food Allergies

Food allergies can be deadly. Knowing about them beforehand is essential. As an example, some people are so extremely sensitive to certain foods, like peanuts, they need their food cooked with utensils, cutting boards, and pots and pans that never come in contact with peanuts. Any trace of peanuts, even peanut *dust*, can lead to serious problems. Some products have warning labels that will alert you if it was manufactured in a location where peanuts have been present.

Food allergies are an immune system response to a food that the body believes is harmful. Once the immune system decides a food is harmful, it manufactures specific antibodies to combat it. The next time that food is ingested, the immune system releases enormous amounts of histamine to protect the body. This triggers a variety of allergic symptoms that can affect the respiratory system, gastrointestinal tract, skin, and/or cardiovascular system.

Where Did You Learn So Much about Food?

I graduated from the California Culinary Academy in San Francisco. It was eighteen months of intense, exciting, and challenging study. After working for several years as a chef, I went to France to what I called "finishing school" at the Ritz Escoffier and at La Varenne in Paris. This taught me how important knowing French culinary technique was. I moved on from there, but the lessons I learned in Paris I still use today.

The personal chefs who contributed their experiences to this book learned about food in many different ways. Jeff Parker owned a cafe and read *How to Start a Home-Based Catering Business* by me (completely unsolicited!). Betsy Rogers started with a nine-week Mastering the Basics class at a local school, followed by two nine-week courses and a weeklong "boot camp" at the Culinary Institute of America (CIA) in Hyde Park, New York. She continually challenges herself to perfect new techniques. Hoyt and Lydia Eells took all the courses offered by the USPCA, along with frequent classes at the Santa Fe Cooking School and many other classes offered through *Chef magazine* (chefmagazine.com).

Monique Porche-Smith went from playing restaurant as a child to an associate's degree in culinary arts from the Institute of Atlanta and is currently pursuing her bachelor's degree in culinary arts management from the same institution. Vicki Brown attended Johnson & Wales University fully intending on becoming a pastry chef. Scott Wilson is self-taught but comes from a long line of great home cooks and has owned his own restaurant. He was certified as an executive chef in 1987 and inducted into the American Academy of Chefs a few years later.

Randy Eckstein's education began in high school with his job as a busboy in a local family restaurant, where he moved up to dishwasher and then prep cook. He worked his way through undergraduate and graduate school with jobs in kitchen management. The culinary part of his education later continued with employment at hotels, private clubs, organic grocers, restaurants, and executive dining rooms.

Reid Smith, who has taken many professional culinary courses, thought it very interesting that at a personal chef conference he attended in 2003, only about one third of the attendees were formally trained.

I also find this information interesting because I was a guest speaker at that very conference. If I was hiring a personal chef, I would love to know that they had studied their craft and were the best they could be. I have found that my clients love hearing about my education, experiences, and travels. My culinary history is part of my sales pitch.

Scientists estimate that about 11 million Americans suffer from food allergies. Avoidance is the only way to prevent an allergic reaction. There is no cure.

Although a person can be allergic to any food, the following eight foods account for 90 percent of all food-allergic reactions: milk, eggs, peanuts, fish, shellfish, soy, wheat, and tree nuts (walnuts, cashews, pecans, almonds, hazelnuts, pistachios, and Brazil nuts). Discuss food allergies with your clients and carefully read labels to avoid cooking food with hidden allergens.

What's That Hiding in Your Food?

I am allergic to soy, so I was alarmed to find that it is added to all sorts of products. This has forced me to be much more careful about reading labels and finding suitable alternatives.

Animal products, allergens, and chemicals can all be hiding in common packaged foods. The list below will give you an idea of how confusing (and sometimes dangerous) food labels can be.

Ingredients that may indicate the presence of soy:

- Gum arabic
- Carob
- Emulsifier
- Guar gum
- Hydrolyzed vegetable protein (HVP)

- Lecithin
- MSG
- Protein
- Stabilizer
- Starch
- Textured vegetable protein (TVP)
- Thickener
- Vegetable broth, gum, or starch

Ingredients that may indicate the presence of peanuts:

- Ground nuts
- Flavoring
- Asian sauce

Ingredients that may indicate the presence of wheat:

- Cornstarch
- Gelatinized starch
- Gluten
- Hydrolyzed vegetable protein
- Modified food starch
- MSG
- Protein
- Starch
- Vegetable gum or starch

Products that may contain peanuts or peanut oil as a hidden ingredient:

- Ice cream
- Margarine
- Marzipan
- Vegetable oil

Below is an ingredient list from a national, well-known food product. See if you can guess what it is by reading the list of ingredients!

> **Ingredients:** MILK, WHEY, MILK PROTEIN CONCENTRATE, WHEY PROTEIN CONCENTRATE, SODIUM PHOSPHATE, MILKFAT, MALTODEXTRIN, DRIED CORN SYRUP, SALT, LACTIC ACID, SORBIC ACID, SODIUM ALGINATE, SODIUM CITRATE, ENZYMES, CHEESE CULTURE, VITAMIN A PALMITATE, APOCAROTENAL, ANNATTO

Answer: *It's Velveeta!*

Your Personal Chef Personality

Your personal chef personality—your PCP, if you will—describes your preference for certain work environments. Realizing your working style will help you decide which clients to market yourself to, which clients to avoid, and what will make you happier in the long run. Which description below describes you best?

- *The Silent Loner*—can't abide distractions. Loves to cook but needs peace and quiet to concentrate. Finds children especially alarming. Tends to be fussy but gets an enormous amount done. Does not need interaction or feedback from clients.
- *The Zen Master*—can create a serene work space in any situation. Is not ruffled by uncertainty and chaos. Is as happy working alone as working around others. Needs minimal feedback, but the occasional thank you is appreciated.
- *The Nurturer*—is happiest when making wholesome, comforting foods. Takes special joy in cooking for children and seniors. Often leaves a plate of cookies or some other treat for clients. Flourishes with frequent positive feedback from clients.
- *The Teacher*—gets the most satisfaction from passing knowledge on to clients. Makes sure initial consults are thorough; looks forward to periodic progress or report card meetings to reassess and adjust services to better fit clients.
- *The Drill Sergeant*—is happiest when keeping people on strict diets. Takes great pleasure in helping people to realize their goals. Loves helping clients go through their cupboards and refrigerator to rid them of all restricted foods. Expects weekly updates to help fine-tune service. Leaves clients' kitchen floors so clean they could eat off them.

- *The Social Chef*—is happiest cooking in the presence of clients. Thrives on interaction, interruption, and a bit of chaos. Doesn't mind at all the extra time this takes and, in fact, enjoys hearing about the client's day. Expects frequent and detailed feedback.

Do you recognize yourself in any of the descriptions? You might be a combination of two or three. Whichever you are, realize what it is you need from your clients to keep *you* happy. And remember, for every personal chef personality type, there is a corresponding client type: a Zen Master will not be happy working with social clients or nurturers who want to hang out and chat while he's working.

Making the Most of Your Talents and Specialties

We all have food preferences and special food knowledge. What are yours? Are you a wonderful baker? Does cooking Italian food satisfy something deep within your soul? Do you relish the challenge of creating delicious meals with low-fat ingredients? Maybe you've tried every popular diet. You don't think of yourself as a constant dieter, but rather as someone who possesses quite a bit of information on the subject of dieting. You have the chance to use your special knowledge to provide a valuable service to potential clients. When selling your services, highlight your talents and specialties, whatever they may be. Having worked with just about every national fitness guru to come down the pike over the last twenty years (either developing their recipes or styling their cookbooks), I've learned tons about healthy cooking. It makes a great addition to my food bag of tricks.

PC Scott Wilson says, "My permanent clients tend to have real needs. The elderly might need support in the kitchen because of a disability or physical limitations. They do not want to leave their homes, so this gives them some support through these trying times. Families tend to be time stressed and just are not eating properly. They want to get the family back to the table and see this service as a means to that end. Individuals and working couples tend to be on various schedules. They find having prepared meals in the home a convenience and a practical way to take care of their dietary needs. Individuals with special needs appreciate the concept of customization of this service. Recipients of gift certificates appreciate the service and hopefully become valued advertising for future personal chef services."

Mike Cesario says he "will take on most clients' dietary restrictions as long as they are able to give me a complete list of foods to either avoid or add to their meals. My one stipulation on these diets is that the client needs to know exactly what is entailed in their program. I will not research something totally on my own that they are just thinking of trying." Mike knows it isn't cost-effective to invest hours of time when it won't lead to more income.

Most of Pauline Reep's clients have hired her because they are tired of eating out. "They want to have a more nutritious lifestyle, and they're in need of better eating habits. I like to say that I help guide them out of their fast-food rut. A lot of my clients want to lose weight, so I will guide them by telling them which dietary parameters might suit them best. My favorite diet has been Weight Watchers, as it instills healthy eating habits but with portion control. I generally will try to keep my clients on the right track by steering them away from fad diets. If they insist on doing the fad diets, I will study the diet and work in the parameters, but it has been my experience that most clients try the fad for one service and then go back to a low-fat/portion-controlled service."

Popular Diets

There are too many special diets to go into great detail about all of them here, but I can give you a brief overview of some of the most popular. These aren't religious- or ethics-based diets or doctor-prescribed diets like the ones we've described earlier. All the diets below have a variety of cookbooks that go along with them. You might find the cookbooks a helpful way to create menus for some of your clients.

Weight Watchers, created by Jean Nidetch and Felice Marks Lippert, enforces healthy, balanced, and sensible eating habits. Point values are assigned to foods, and food is consumed within these set limits. All foods are allowed in moderation.

The Atkins Diet, created by Dr. Robert Atkins, is a very low-carb, high-protein diet that promises quick results. You will be cooking with a lot of meat, bacon, eggs, cheese, butter, and nuts. Not good for vegetarians or people with high cholesterol.

The South Beach Diet, created by Dr. Arthur Agatston, also offers quick results. This low-carb diet balances certain fats and carbs. Clients on this diet will eat lots of lean meat, poultry, fish, shellfish, eggs, low-fat or fat-free cheese, most fruits, some breads, pastas, and brown rice. The downside is the many rules you have to follow.

The Zone Diet, created by Dr. Barry Sears, has dieters consuming a 40/30/30 percent balance of carbs, protein, and fats at every meal. Weight loss is slower and steadier than with the low-carb diets above and this diet is favored by athletes wanting to gain lean muscle mass. The Zone Diet will require you to cook lots of seafood, poultry, lean meats, fruits, most vegetables, and nuts. The downside to this diet is the even larger number of rules than the South Beach Diet. This is a particularly difficult diet for PCs because they usually just provide dinners, and this diet demands an overall balance among all meals.

How This Book Is Organized

Will you make mistakes? Absolutely! But from this book you'll gain an excellent overview of what working as a personal chef requires, along with signposts marking the various pitfalls. You'll learn what the traits of a good personal chef are, what your personal chef style is, and how best to work with your special talents and knowledge. I feel that my success stems from playing to my strengths and talents. I'm a whiz at sales and food production, but small talk when I'm cooking isn't my strong point—I prefer to leave my clients notes.

I'll give you the tools to get you organized, the knowledge to keep your food safe, the importance of a business plan, and where to go for help and inspiration. Chapter 4 is devoted to legal matters pertaining to providing personal chef services. Chapter 6 focuses on marketing your services, and chapter 7 is about organizing your day. Chapter 8 gives you information on how to make a profit, how to organize your business, and how to increase your income stream. And, in chapter 9, I give you menus and recipes to cover nearly any style of eating.

This book will help you to make as few mistakes as possible. But keep in mind that the only real mistake is the lesson you fail to learn from. The world is your oyster—go cook it!

02

Creating a Kitchen to Go

There are many ways to carry your cooking kit: in plastic tubs, canvas tote bags, milk crates, toolboxes, etc. You need to pack your supplies in a way that allows you to easily lift and carry them without straining. A small wheeled cart can make life easier, but it won't help you if you need to climb stairs. You should be able to pick up and carry every piece you pack. I've always gone with smaller square crates lined with plastic bags. I may haul more of them, but depending on the size of the kitchen I am working in, I can stack them vertically and keep them out of my way when cooking. And they're cheap and easy to clean.

If you have a long way to drive, a small refrigerator that runs off your car battery or a cooler will add to the shelf life of delicate products. A medium-size cooler on wheels is also a good idea. I bought one recently at a local BevMo for $26. Ice packs will keep things cool all day or overnight, but if you are only storing items for an hour or so, simply putting cold items in a cooler will keep them cool just fine.

Getting Ready

Depending on what you already own, count on spending a few hundred dollars on creating your kitchen to go. I've created lists (see page 20) to help you start your personal chef kit. If you've been in culinary school or done any catering, you'll notice that many of the listed items are already in your toolbox. Decide what carrying containers work for you. It's nice to be able to leave your kit and your toolbox in your car at the end of each day. If you've put your kit away clean, there is no need to unload it when you get home.

One place to start assembling your kit is from your own cupboards. The equipment you'll need will be determined by the food and menus your clients request, so we are talking about a general kit here. But if it's been months or years since you cleaned out your kitchen cupboards, you might be surprised at what you already own. You probably have a plastic colander or a set of plastic mixing bowls that you've forgotten about. I suggest plastic whenever you can make it work, for three simple reasons: Plastic is lighter, easier to carry, and unbreakable. Everything on my list (except for knives) is dishwasher safe. You want to be able to wash and sanitize equipment in your client's dishwasher at the end of each cooking day.

Getting Your Clients Ready

After organizing your own kitchen, you'll be ready to move on to those of your clients. I know you're thinking, "Is that really my job—to clean out their cabinets?" The answer is *yes*. Think of it as part of your service. It's best to know what your clients already have, and by making room in their cabinets, you have space for any disposables you want to leave there. This helps you to make everything run more smoothly right from the start.

One of the clients I cooked for in Malibu bought several sets of beautiful covered ovenproof serving dishes that I continually filled. They went from the stove to the refrigerator, back to the oven, to the dinner table, and back to the refrigerator. They even went in the freezer. The client felt it was better for the environment to avoid disposables, and I had no problem with it.

I also suggest that you start cheap. Don't go out and buy expensive equipment. Find out what works for your clients before you spend money. Some of them might prefer you to use their equipment. You won't know until you meet with them. Maybe your clientele will all want grilled chicken breasts and steamed vegetables. Wait and see, and buy as you need.

Some personal chefs feel comfortable using their clients' pots and pans; others don't. It's really up to you, what you've discussed with your clients, and, to be honest, the state of their pots and pans. When clients need pots and pans, I often suggest a set I know is on sale or is a great buy at a discount warehouse store like Costco or Sam's Club. Depending on the client, I might offer to purchase these for them because I like shopping with other people's money.

It's also good to educate your clients about quality cookware, knives, or bone china. If well taken care of, these pieces will last them a lifetime.

Outfitting Your Portable Kitchen

Most personal chefs bring everything they need with them, including their own cleaning supplies. (See page 20 to get you started.)

Speak to your clients, and work out the details of your service with each of them on a client-to-client basis. I've had the best of both worlds: kitchens where I didn't bring a thing and everything was supplied, and kitchens where I brought everything I needed down to the box of toothpicks. Personally, I prefer the former because I found all the lifting and carrying harder than the actual cooking.

Pots and Pans: Used versus New

There are many places to buy equipment for your portable kitchen. Restaurant-quality cookware is available at restaurant supply stores (check the phone book), auctions, out-of-business sales (check your local newspaper listings), and online. Good-quality cookware for the general consumer can be purchased new at department store sales or at online discounters like Overstock.com or Half.com. As a member of a culinary organization like the International Association of Culinary Professionals or Women Chefs and Restaurateurs, you can get a 15 to 30 percent discount from cookware and appliance manufacturers when you shop online. An excellent source for new or slightly used cookware and appliances is eBay, as are

Portable Kitchen Checklist

Starting basics

- Two 12-inch nonstick skillets (one with lid)
- One 4-quart saucepan with lid
- One cast-iron grill pan
- One Dutch oven with lid
- Two (or more) plastic cutting boards
- Disposable cutting mats to use over the top of your cutting boards
- Stainless-steel or plastic mixing bowls
- Plastic colander
- Fine mesh strainer
- Four nonstick baking sheets with sides
- Wire cooling rack
- Roasting pan
- Hand mixer
- Immersion blender
- Food processor (mini size works for most things)

Disposables to leave at client's home:

- Aluminum foil
- Plastic wrap
- Gallon- and quart-size freezer bags
- Disposables for finished meals

Your toolbox

- Knives with knife guards
- Spatulas for turning and scraping
- Tongs
- Spoons
- Instant-read thermometer
- Scissors
- Whisk
- Measuring cups and spoons
- Can opener
- Wine opener
- Vegetable peeler
- Zester
- Potato masher
- Microplane grater and regular grater
- Two kitchen timers
- Kitchen twine

Your cleaning kit (carry this in a big bucket with a handle). If you have regular long-term clients, ask to leave a cleaning kit in their home.

- Liquid dish soap
- Dishwasher soap packets
- Rubber gloves
- Scrub brush or sponge
- Grease-cutting kitchen cleaner
- Glass cleaner
- Antibacterial cleaner
- Paper towels
- Garbage bags

weekly papers devoted to classifieds, like the *Recycler* (which is also online). Many people use the *Recycler* or eBay to unload items for which they no longer have a use but that are essential to your business.

Always clean new and used cookware thoroughly before using it. There is nothing wrong with purchasing used pots and pans as long as their condition is good. That being said, I would not advise buying used nonstick pans because they become less effective with age, and most people do not care properly for them.

Some additional places to purchase equipment are estate sales, swap meets, and storage companies that sell unclaimed items.

The Importance of a Good Knife

James Beard said, "Knives are the best friends a cook can have, to be treasured along with the family silver." A well-designed knife becomes an extension of your hand, cutting through food as if it were butter. A sharp knife is safer than a dull knife because it will slip less.

There are four basic knives that chefs find invaluable: the chef's knife, the paring knife, the boning knife, and the serrated knife. You may find a boning knife unnecessary if you buy meats already boned.

Membership in a culinary organization can get you a 20 percent (or more) discount on a wide variety of culinary products, including knives. If you bring your business card into your local Sur La Table store, they will put you in their system as a culinary professional. This will get you a 15 percent discount on their merchandise.

A good chef's knife or a (even more popular) santoku will be your most-used knife. An 8-inch knife is the most common, but you may find that a longer or shorter knife will be more comfortable for you. A good serrated knife and a paring knife will round out your knife set, at least initially. Chefs love their knives and often have many more. Knives to chefs are like shoes to women. The more we have, the better we feel.

A steel to keep your knife honed is essential, as are knife guards to keep you from cutting yourself and to keep the edges from getting dull. You should also find a good place to have your knives sharpened once or twice a year.

Basic Knife Cuts

The knife cuts shown on the next page are the professional standard. When following recipes, it is good to know exactly what size "small dice" or "julienne" is. Not

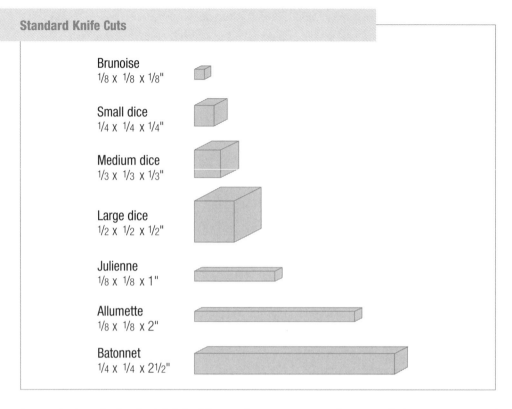

Brunoise
1/8 x 1/8 x 1/8"

Small dice
1/4 x 1/4 x 1/4"

Medium dice
1/3 x 1/3 x 1/3"

Large dice
1/2 x 1/2 x 1/2"

Julienne
1/8 x 1/8 x 1"

Allumette
1/8 x 1/8 x 2"

Batonnet
1/4 x 1/4 x 2 1/2"

only does the finished dish look better if your cuts are uniform, it will also come out better, because any recipe you make will have been written with these sizes in mind. Uniform shapes also allow for even cooking.

Dry Pantry Ingredients to Always Have on Hand

There are some items that you will want to have in your kit (or portable kitchen), your kitchen, or your client's kitchen. Of course, these ingredients will depend on the kind of meals you are preparing, but here's a general list:

- Canola oil
- Olive oil
- Nonstick cooking spray
- Sea salt or kosher salt
- Peppercorns in a peppermill
- Stone ground mustard

- Dijon mustard
- Soy sauce
- Tomato sauce
- Crushed tomatoes
- Tomato paste
- Good-quality low-sodium chicken broth
- Variety of pasta
- Variety of rice
- Honey
- Sugar
- Flour
- Cornstarch
- Vanilla extract
- Selection of spices and dried herbs
- Panko breadcrumbs
- Balsamic vinegar
- Apple cider vinegar
- Red wine vinegar

Food Safety

Have you ever eaten and a few hours later you've felt queasy? The culprit was probably unseen bacteria from improperly handled food. Food contamination and the resulting food poisoning can pose serious health problems. If you've ever suffered from a bout of food poisoning, you know that this is something you should take every precaution to avoid. It will pretty much end a relationship with a client.

Wash Your Hands

Without getting into the gory details about the risks of contracting hepatitis A or staphylococcus, let's just say that personal hygiene and thorough hand washing are a must in any kitchen. Follow these commonsense rules to ensure your food is safe:

- Wash hands before, during, and after handling food, preferably with an antibacterial soap and a nailbrush.
- Wash hands after using the restroom, smoking, coughing, sneezing, or scratching.

- Tie your hair back or wear a hat so you don't leave hair in the food.
- Cover any cuts on your hands with bandages, and wear disposable latex gloves.
- Put on a new pair of gloves when you've handled raw meats to avoid cross-contamination.
- Don't use your fingers to taste your creations. Disposable plastic spoons are ideal for this purpose.

Keep Your Work Area Clean

Keeping your work area clean will reduce the risk of contamination. Always scrub cutting boards with hot soapy water when switching from one kind of food (raw chicken) to another (fruit). Wash counters and work surfaces with an antibacterial cleanser before and after you cook.

Get into the habit of cleaning pots, pans, and dishes as you go. This is a restaurant technique that will help keep things running smoothly and make cleanup at the end easier.

Handling Leftovers

Leftover food should be cooled quickly, placed in airtight containers, and refrigerated as soon as possible. Leftovers should be reheated to a temperature of at least 165°F to destroy any bacteria that has taken up residence. Refrigerated meals should be eaten within three days. If they are not going to be consumed in that time, they should be frozen.

Be Careful What You Buy

When you buy meats or other high-protein foods (milk products, cream, cheese, or tofu), always check the "use by" date. Beef, veal, and lamb should be red and fresh looking. If ground meat has a gray tone, then it was ground days ago and is not fresh.

Fish should smell like the sea; if it's fishy smelling, it isn't fresh. When buying whole fish, the eyes should be clear and shiny. Look for a red or pink color around the gills and shiny scales. When pressed, fish should be firm and elastic; it should not dent easily. You will most likely be buying your fish in filets or steaks, so you must rely on your sense of smell for freshness. If in doubt, don't buy it.

Working Efficiently in a Cramped Kitchen

A small kitchen and limited counter space need not hamper you. Here are some helpful hints and tips for you to maximize your work space.

- Create extra surface space. Place a cooling rack or baking sheet across your sink for more work space. Use a kitchen drawer pulled out and covered with a tray.

- If your kitchen does not have shelving space, put up a unit that comes "ready to install." Use wall-mounted racks or baskets for storage and a Peg-Board on your wall to hang stainless steel bowls, pots, pans, and cooking utensils.

- When making large batches of something that require refrigeration on baking sheets (truffles, cookies, etc.), it is better to stack the baking sheets alternately, turning them every other way so they are not exactly on top of each other. If you need to stack bowls in the refrigerator in order to fit everything, put plates in between the bowls, don't rely on plastic wrap alone to hold tight. Make sure it is a safe, non slippery surface. If it seems slippery, put a towel in between the layers for stability.

- Tape recipes you are using at eye level on the fridge or on kitchen cabinets so they aren't cluttering the counters.

- Keep a trashcan or bucket handy for quick and easy disposal. Fill your sink or a large bowl with soapy water, and put dirty dishes, bowls, and utensils in it as you go so they don't pile up.

Cross-Contamination

Keep your packages of raw meat separate from produce. Drips from meat packages contain bacteria that, if not washed off, could cause someone to get very sick.

This transfer of bacteria is called cross-contamination and is responsible for many outbreaks of food poisoning. If you use a cutting board to prepare raw chicken, do not use the same board to cut lettuce unless it has first been thoroughly washed with hot soapy water.

Many personal chefs use different-colored plastic cutting boards for specific types of food. They use a red cutting board for raw meats and green for fruits and vegetables. Some even have cutting boards specifically for fish or for garlic.

There is quite a cutting board controversy going on currently. After reading the pros and cons and using every type of cutting board there is, my preference is plastic. Critics of plastic say they are not good because plastic flakes can end up in the food. Critics of wood say they are not good because bacteria hides deep in the pores of the wood and can never be truly cleaned.

I run my plastic cutting boards through the dishwasher; this assures me that they are clean. Wood boards warp and take a lot of special care. Professional kitchens run cutting boards through soapy water containing a mild bleach solution (bleach solutions are always 1 part bleach to 10 parts water). If you don't know what you are doing, you can use too much bleach and it will get in the food. Sometimes you just have to pick your poison.

Food Storage and Handling

There are two reasons for proper storage: sanitation and money. Holding food at the proper temperature and in the proper container will keep it from getting dried out and from spoiling. You want your food to last as long as possible in the best condition as possible. Here are guidelines for you to follow when storing food:

- Plan your grocery-shopping trip so that perishables are unrefrigerated for the least amount of time. You may want to consider taking a cooler packed with ice or ice packs if you have delicate items that need to be refrigerated. A cooler will also come in handy if you are shopping in the middle of summer or the ride home is a long one. You can also use the ice for ice baths to cool food later in the day.
- Proper refrigeration at all times is the key to preserving freshness and keeping bacteria at bay. Perishables must be kept at 41°F or less and frozen food at 32°F or less. The ideal temperature for bacteria to thrive is 41°–140°F. This is known as *the temperature danger zone*. The longer food stays in this zone, the higher the bacterial count will be. After four hours (in total), food should no longer be considered edible.
- A simple rule to remember is to keep cold foods cold and hot foods hot.

- Do not let foods, especially protein, sit out unprotected; cover with plastic wrap.
- Store all food in well-sealed storage containers.
- Raw food should be stored away from food that does not get cooked, like fruit or lettuce. Raw meats should be kept in the lower part of the refrigerator where they cannot drip onto other food.
- Refrigerate cooked food immediately. Pour hot foods into pans that are no more than 2 inches deep. Stirring large pans occasionally while they cool will hasten the cooling process. Setting hot pans in an ice bath will cool a large stockpot faster and safer. Contrary to popular opinion, letting food cool at room temperature merely allows it to spend longer in the bacteria-breeding range of 41°–140°F.
- Placing hot food directly into the refrigerator without cooling it will only raise the temperature of the refrigerator, which is not good for everything else in the fridge.

Freezing and Thawing

All your wonderful cooking will be for naught if you don't properly store your creations. Here are some tips for successfully freezing and thawing:

- In order to prevent any bacteria from growing, it is important to chill cooked food before freezing. This also reduces the collection of excess moisture

Temperature Danger Zone Chart

Poultry and stuffed meats	165°F	Reheating foods
Pork and ground meats	155°F	
Eggs	145°F	
Keep hot foods above	140°F	
	↕	**Danger zone**
Keep cold foods below	41°F	
Preferred cold food storage	41°–32°F	
Keep frozen foods below	32°F	

Thermometers Are Your Friends

There are four basic types of kitchen-essential thermometers: meat thermometers, candy or deep-fat frying thermometers, oven thermometers, and refrigerator or freezer thermometers. Thermometers precisely measure the doneness and cooking temperatures of foods as well as guarantee that refrigerators, freezers, and ovens are operating efficiently.

To calibrate a thermometer, or check the accuracy of the temperature reading, boil a pot of water. For an instant-read thermometer, stick it in the water for twenty seconds; for a meat or candy thermometer, stick it in the water for three minutes. They should both read 212°F, which is the boiling temperature of water. If the instant-read does not read 212°F, twist the face of the dial until it reads 212°F. If the meat or candy thermometer does not read 212°F, calculate the difference and make the proper recipe adjustments.

Meat Thermometers. There are two types to choose from: a regular meat thermometer and an instant-read thermometer. Regular meat thermometers are inserted into the meat at the beginning of the cooking process and are left there while cooking until the appropriate temperature of the meat is reached. Insert half of the probe into the thickest part of the meat, avoiding bone or gristle. Instant-read thermometers are inserted at numerous times during the cooking process and in different parts of the food to ensure the correct cooking temperature is being met. Insert about 2 inches of the probe into the meat source and leave it in there for twenty seconds or until the temperature stabilizes.

Candy or Deep-Fat Frying Thermometers. The most common type is an easy-to-read glass tube with a bulb at the end and an adjustable clip for attaching to pots and pans. Immerse the thermometer upright into the oil or other liquid, making sure the bulb of the thermometer does not touch the bottom of the pot or pan. Leave in place until the temperature reading stabilizes.

Oven Thermometers. There are two basic types of oven thermometers: mercury-style glass tubes and spring-operated dial thermometers. The mercury-style glass tubes give more accurate readings than the spring-operated dial. To use this thermometer, place it on the middle rack of an oven at a temperature of 350°F for fifteen minutes. It should then read 350°F. If it doesn't, calculate the temperature difference and make the proper recipe adjustments.

Refrigerator and Freezer Thermometers. Place the thermometer near the top and front of the appliance. Let it sit for six hours or overnight. Refrigerators should read 40°F and freezers should read 0°F or below. If they don't, adjust the appliance and test it again to ensure an accurate temperature.

because the food is no longer steaming when placed in the freezer. Excess moisture in frozen food equals watery, soggy food when reheated.

- The best way to cool food quickly is to place containers of hot food into an ice bath. Also, metal containers cool much faster than plastic. I often place soup pots directly on ice and can usually get my food cool in about thirty minutes so it's ready for the fridge or freezer.
- Remove excess air from freezer bags and containers to prevent freezer burn.
- If using plastic wrap or bags, go for the heavy-duty kind. Sometimes the packaging will say "microwave plastic." Thin or flimsy plastic will allow too much air in, causing freezer burn.
- If your client is concerned about plastic in the microwave, let them know they can defrost from the freezer (overnight in the fridge), then heat up their food either on a plate or bowl that is made of glass, Pyrex, etc. They can cover the food with a paper towel to insulate the heat and prevent any microwave "splatters".
- Use the smallest possible container to cut down the amount of air the food comes in contact with.
- Be sure to label frozen food clearly, with date made as well as a "best by" date.
- For optimum quality, thaw frozen foods in the refrigerator for a few hours or overnight.

- Two alternative thawing methods are to run cold water over food that is tightly wrapped in plastic or to use the microwave at the defrost setting. These methods of thawing must be followed with immediate cooking.

Each new client you attain will require a bit of educating on defrosting, thawing, and reheating their meals. Take your time to explain clearly and, before you know it, your client will be trained on how best to enjoy your food; you will become indispensable!

Smart Purchasing: Get to Know Your Local Grocers

Some grocers will offer a 10 to 15 percent discount just for seeing your business license.

Some smaller retailers will give you discounts, but you must approach them. Tell them about your business and how much money you plan to be spending on a regular basis. It never hurts to ask.

The biggest advantage to knowing local grocers or wholesalers is having them point you toward the best produce or alert you to special deals. Much of this is simply making the most of what's in season. When salmon is plentiful, try to serve it to all your clients. Put it on the menu and sell it. Buying in season will save you money.

Working with Suppliers

Most personal chefs, including you, will purchase their groceries (meats, fish, produce) and other supplies at a regular grocery store. However, as time goes on, you will discover that you may no longer want to buy food at retail prices. Because you are in business for yourself and your goal is to make money, it may make more sense for you to purchase many of your dry goods or volume items from discount stores like Costco.

If you bill your clients for the groceries separately from your service fee, as many chefs do, then you might not care what you spend on groceries, but if you charge one price for your food and your service, it will behoove you to save as much money on raw product as possible. You must control your food cost to make more profit. The less you pay and the more you charge are the dynamics that run profit. Speak to every manager in every store. Show them how much money you will be spending weekly, monthly, yearly. Ask for discounts. This could save you 10 to 20 percent, resulting in more profit to you.

Your next step is to research small wholesale purveyors in your area and visit their warehouses. You may be able to purchase some things by the case price but only take one or two items from the case, storing the remainder in their refrigerator or warehouse. This is referred to as "breaking a case." Another way to find out about quality purveyors is to ask other personal chefs whom they recommend.

It is crucial to have a good working relationship with the managers of your local stores and sales representatives for purveyors. This can save you time in designing menus, controlling food costs, and solving food production problems. It is the job of sales reps to know current portions, shelf life, and availability of special seasonal items. Use what they know; it's less work for you!

Chefs typically have a number of purveyors who specialize in different goods: one purveyor for dry goods, one for produce, one for seafood, and one for meats. This way you can save time, money, and gas by placing almost all of your orders over the phone.

If you do most of your purchasing from a local grocery store, have the manager of the meat counter get all your poultry and meat for each client ready the day before you need it so you can whiz by and pick it up on the way to the client's home (see sample order form on page 33).

You'll need to check the rules of your local health department about food storage. Some counties and states will not allow personal chefs to store any perishables anyplace other than the client's home.

When I was a personal chef, I was able to get my produce delivered to each client's home the morning I cooked there from a family-owned produce market. I faxed them an order form and a delivery schedule the week before, along with the clients' addresses. Most of the produce was for sides and salads, so if there was a short sup-ply of something, I could make do with substitutions. Having a long-term relation-ship with your purveyors guarantees that you will get the finest-quality foods and enables you to negotiate prices, suggest alternative products, and provide timely and safe packaging and delivery.

Great relationships with your purveyors can even get you leads on jobs and tips on creative presentation and menu ideas. As we often say in the trade, you're only as good as your purveyors. Make sure you find the best!

The Next Step

In the next chapter you have homework. I want you to write down your thoughts, hopes, and goals. You can think of it as a business plan (which it is), but if that seems like too much work or just plain overwhelming, call it a business diary. The idea is to have a place to organize all the information you gather so that you can figure out what to do with it and how to use it.

I know many of you will want to skip this step. You want to cook, not write. In the planning stages of any business, the success is in the details. The time and energy you put into researching this satisfying career will help you build for long-term suc-cess and financial gain.

Jennifer's
Personal Chef Service

310-555-1234

Butchery Order Form

Store: _____

Pickup time: _____   Date order placed: _____

MONDAY	TUESDAY	WEDNESDAY	THURSDAY	FRIDAY
Client:_____	Client:_____	Client:_____	Client:_____	Client:_____
2 lbs. ground beef, lean	4 salmon filets 5 oz. each	2 lbs. ground turkey, lean	4 pork loin chops, 5 oz.	2 lbs. chuck roast
1½ lbs. bay shrimp	6 Italian turkey sausages	2 lbs. ground beef, lean	1½ lbs. large sea scallops	2 lbs. ground beef, lean
4 boneless chicken breasts 5–6 oz. each	1 whole chicken about 3 lbs.	4 bone-in chicken breasts 6–7 oz. each	4 boneless chicken breasts about 3 lbs.	1 turkey breast about 4 lbs.
2 lbs. ground pork shoulder	½ lb. ground beef, lean	2 lbs. large shrimp, deveined	½ lb. ground beef, lean	1 lb. stewing meat

03

Business Plan for the Personal Chef

A business plan is the document that helps you express your plans for your business, both immediate and long term. It is a great way to gather all your thoughts and ideas about what you expect and organize them in one place—lining up all your ducks, in other words.

You won't create a business plan in a couple of days. In fact, in my catering classes, I give my students the entire semester to get it together. No one wants to take the time. I hear lots of grumbling and groaning. What I say to them is, "You can't afford *not* to do it." How can you get to where you want to go if you don't have a clear idea of "where" is?

Writing a business plan is the single best way to create a written vision of your business. You will be able to measure your success against it, and it is an important tool to help you make decisions.

Writing a Business Plan

Having a descriptive business plan is an important part of organizing not only your new business but also your thoughts, hopes, and dreams. Having it all written down will keep you on track. And it will also make you consider all aspects of this business, many of which you probably weren't aware of. A business plan will make you consider the long term of your success in this business. Answer these questions, flesh out the sections, and you will have a great start on a business plan. If you can't answer these questions, start seeking the answers. Most businesses fail because of surprises, not lack of opportunities.

Step 1: The Summary Statement

- Your name and the primary location (city) where you will be working.
- Who you are and what your credentials are.
- The market(s) you plan to reach, without limiting yourself to that market.
- What it is that makes you different from the competition? Specify a few of the most important things that make you stand out from everybody else in this business. Have you checked out the competition in your area?
- Can your community support another personal chef? How many is it supporting right now?

Step 2: Type of Ownership

Typically, a personal chef business is a sole proprietorship. Other types of businesses include limited liability corporations (LLCs), but these are not generally used for personal chef services. If your business grows and you move into a commercial kitchen, add catering services to your business, or find yourself hiring employees, a sole proprietorship may no longer suit your legal needs. It also depends on what assets you have. If you've got nothing, you've got nothing to protect. If you own property and don't want to lose it in a possible product liability lawsuit, I suggest you speak to your accountant and attorney and ask them "How should I hold the title or structure my business?"

I ran my business successfully for years as a sole proprietorship. As it and my assets grew, my accountant (I cherish him) and my attorney (the best husband I've ever had) advised me to incorporate. It was easy. I called a company that offers incorporation services, and voila, I was incorporated. The cost was minimal. I also have many students and personal chefs that have done the paperwork themselves.

Being a corporation makes your bookkeeping slightly more complicated. My advice is to befriend a good accountant.

As a sole proprietor, you are the owner, boss, and head chef, as well as the marketing department, bookkeeper, dishwasher, and ambassador of goodwill.

You will learn to juggle all these different hats and (hopefully) enjoy them.

Step 3: Defining Your Niche and Competition

- Are there other personal chefs in your area? If so, what do they specialize in? How are you different from them in what they do and who they cook for? Get all the information you can about your competition. Can you see or develop a niche in your community that no one has yet touched on?
- Are there restaurants or catering companies in your area that offer personal chef services that may have an edge up on you and your clientele? How can you compete with them? Or, could you introduce yourself to them and find out if there is a way to market your services through them?
- What type of meal-assembly centers are in your area? These companies may steal potential or existing clients from you. The big players are Dream Dinners, Supper's Ready, and Let's Dish, but they aren't the only ones. I heard from several personal chefs that as these franchises had opened in their neighborhoods, clients wanted to try them and see if they could save money and get the same quality they were getting from personal chef services. It's certainly not a personal chef service. Several years ago, the *New York Times* reported that an average of forty centers a month were opening across the country. They got a tremendous amount of coverage. Most of them didn't make it. There are a few still open but they never took off the way the owners had hoped. They found that consumers really don't want to go to a location and assemble their own meals.
- Are you planning on being only a personal chef or increasing your income stream with catering gigs and special events as well? Define your boundaries as a personal chef. How little or how much do you plan on working?

- Do you specialize in any international cuisines, health or diet foods, gourmet cooking, baking, everyday/easy food, comfort food, or a little of everything? Define your specialty niche(s).
- With that said, who do you plan on targeting as your clientele? The health conscious, the wealthy, the middle class, businesspeople, single parents, the elderly, families on the go, or those with special medical concerns? Without totally limiting yourself to a single clientele, have an idea of whom you are going after so you know how to market yourself and your business. I would tap into my entire network for potential clients.

  An example: Say you are a supervising nurse who has worked for fifteen years at a local hospital and you want to make a change. You might have 200 people you've been working with on a regular basis. Make fliers and pass them out, cut down your hours to part-time to keep your benefits, and start your personal chef business. Your fellow coworkers already know and trust you.

  Furthermore, does your target market actually exist in your area? If so, continue research on how to reach your market; if not, reconsider your target market and develop one that relates to the demographics of your area.
- Are people spending their disposable income on nonessential services? Is the personal chef business booming, or is it in a slump? Again, this can also determine your clientele and the target market you are trying to reach.
- Make a name for yourself in your area and community by developing relationships that can help get your name out there. Meet people who can use your services. Increase your exposure so people begin to know who you are and what you do (especially if you are doing good works in your community). In the food world, referral business is critical and should be nurtured.

Step 4: The Difference between Personal Chefs and Caterers

- Caterers are hired for a single job or occasion. PCs are hired on a weekly or monthly basis, which allows you to get to know your clients' tastes very well.
- Food is prepared on-site, in the client's home rather than in an off-site kitchen. You are the only person handling your client's food.

- Because food is prepared in the client's home, your overhead is kept to a minimum, and you pass this savings on to your customers. Caterers have a surcharge for the cost of using professional kitchens.
- Because this is a personalized service, your clients can and will request specific foods or diets from you. Caterers do not want to alter their menus for a client they may only have once.
- Why is this important? The laws, taxes, marketing, and accounting are different for caterers and personal chefs. You are going to have to learn about all of these details. I discuss most of them in this book.

Step 5: Organizing Your Business

- If you work alone, never take more jobs than you can handle. If the money is good enough for you to be able to support yourself, keep the clients that you cook for on a regular basis and whom you know you can count on for regular work. Only say yes to the people and jobs you know you can take on. Do your clients understand your policies, payment schedule, fees, and services? Do they understand that you cook in their kitchens? I've gotten more than one frantic phone call from a personal chef who, upon arriving at the client's home, discovered the kitchen was being remodeled! The client assumed that the personal chef could simply cook the food somewhere else. Laws and insurance don't allow that.
- What will you do if you lose a client? How will you pay your bills? Always have a backup plan. It's best to start every business with at least six months of expenses in the bank. With that said, I didn't have more than a wish and a prayer when I started my first business, but I did learn the art of deposits. And you will too.
- In the event that you have more work than you can handle and you need to hire someone to help you prep or cook, make sure you inform the client of your help's credentials and culinary history, and why you are using him or her for that occasion. It is more honorable of you and your business to pay someone out of your own paycheck to help you during this busy time than to flake out on a client, especially at the last minute when they may not be able to find someone to replace you. Try to establish a reciprocal relationship with another personal chef in your area. If you have joined any of the organizations

suggested in appendix D, you might find a business friend in a chat room or discussion forum. Sharing information strengthens everyone's business.

Step 6: Describing Your Management and Operation

- In your personal bio, emphasize your special talents and include an updated resume. Your bio and resume should include whom you've cooked for (especially if they are big names) and their special dietary needs (if any), what cuisines you specialize in (if any), your culinary training and background (whether professional or nonprofessional: play it up!), years of experience in the culinary field, places you've cooked (especially if you've worked at a big name restaurant or hotel), years of experience in the business industry (which may illustrate to potential clients that you not only know how to cook but you have business savvy and know how to run your own business), and anything else you think may help your chances of gaining a potential client. Include whatever sets you apart from the competition in your area.

- Research how you legally go about having your own personal chef business and how you get a license and permit to be able to run a safe, sanitary, health-regulated business. Determine whether you will be cooking in your client's kitchen or in a rented catering kitchen and what equipment you will need to run your business. Also determine what kind of office you will be working out of—whether a home office or an office space—and what kind of office equipment and supplies you will need.

- One of the interesting things you will discover while working on your business plan is that the laws and regulations regarding personal chefs are not the same *anywhere*. As a matter of fact, the industry is still so new that many government offices are at a loss when you ask them for information. Some cities and states will require you to apply for a business license; some won't. Stay in touch with local government offices in your town. It's always better to know the score.

- Stay organized by developing an operating plan based on a day-by-day, week-by-week, or month-by-month schedule that shows you when jobs start and end. This makes for more efficient scheduling and may protect you against burnout. If you have cook dates five days a week, what day do you take care of your accounting and office work?

Step 7: Developing Your Marketing Plan

- Once you've created a name and business for yourself, work toward referrals and word-of-mouth based on your good reputation to do the advertising for you. Not only is it free, but it's also the most effective selling tool a personal chef can use. Remember that bad word-of-mouth travels ten times faster than good, so run your business wisely and ethically.

- There are thousands of ways to market. The first question to ask yourself is: What kind of marketer are you? Do you like talking on the phone, or are you an e-mail person? Would you like to teach some free classes at a local Whole Foods in order to meet prospective clients or does the idea of speaking to a group make you want to melt into the floor? There is no "right" way to market yourself, but I do believe you must be comfortable and confident in the marketing you do present. People can smell fear, or apathy, a mile away.

- The hottest marketing trend in our industry today is the food blog. The beauty of this is that your blog can be whatever you want it to be: recipes only, personal stories of why you love food, healthy living tips . . . the choice is yours. For the cost of a domain name, and perhaps some Web design assistance if you want to get fancy, you can have a living, breathing business card that is your food blog! I know many successful personal chefs whose only marketing actions were to write their blog, update it regularly, and post it on Facebook and Twitter.

- If social media is new to you, start by simply finding a few food blogs that you enjoy, and tailor your site after theirs. You can also opt to have a more formal website on a blog platform, which will cost you much less than having someone else design you a site from scratch, and you also control all aspects of the site. Both Blogger and WordPress have grown leaps and bounds in being user-friendly, and if you get stuck, just Google your query and a million free tutorials pop up. What will they think of next?

- Having said all that, there is nothing wrong with more traditional marketing. Here are some other avenues to consider: Begin advertising by giving friends and relatives your business cards to hand out. Leave a stack at health clubs and beauty/barber shops in your area. Ask if you can leave some at the doctor's office, country club, church, and/or community centers. In other words, start with the people and places with which you already have a relationship.

- When you start making enough money to advertise, make a postcard with a recipe on it and mail it out to target residences in your area and community. I do this monthly or quarterly in my business. Postcards are a great way to stay in touch with existing clients, solicit new clients, and sell an idea. They also require the cheapest postage and, if they provide a recipe or helpful hints, busy people may want to keep them.

- When marketing yourself, include what kind of services you offer (just personal cheffing or some special events catering too?) and what types of cuisines or diet cooking you specialize in.

- You may want to include how you charge for your services: Do you charge a day rate or an hourly rate? How do you charge for different services? Do you charge shopping time as well? Do you set up payment plans?

- In conclusion, the point of marketing is to make new friends. Let people know who you are and what service you want to provide, and then stay in contact to show that you are around and you are a prolific personal chef. That may mean sending a monthly e-newsletter, or thank-you cards after a job, or birthday wishes with a special discount. Consistent contact will yield excellent results!

Step 8: Creating Your Menus and Website

- A portfolio of recipes or sample menus is the strongest marketing tool you can have. Provide potential clients with sample recipes and pictures and menus of dishes that you have prepared for previous clients. Describe the dishes so well that people can practically taste them; make them want the food right then and there so that they hire you on the spot. We call this "selling the sizzle."

- If you have a signature item, specialty dish, or something extraordinary that sets you apart from the competition, play it up to create a need with potential clients. Also, if you specialize in a current trend or fad such as sushi, raw food, or low-carb diets, include that as well.

- When creating a menu, keep in mind what foods freeze well and what foods don't.

Personal Chef Specialties

Most personal chefs cook whatever their clients ask for. But some personal chefs find that there is a want or need in their community for particular styles of food. Laura Cotton focuses on gourmet and ethnic cuisine. She especially likes Asian dishes, not only for the flavor and health aspects but also because she finds the sauce protects the food during the freezing process. Sandy Hall targets clients with special diets. Marcie McCutchen cooks out of a commercial kitchen and offers online ordering, something that has allowed her to expand her personal chef business into catering.

Betsy Rogers points out that all her dishes are made from scratch. As a result, she finds clients that stay with her a long time and refer her to family and friends. Carlin Breinig's business name is Home Cooking, a name that reflects her specialty: old-fashioned comfort food. Cathy Marella-Luce specializes in gluten-free and dairy-free diets. Linda Simon's tagline is "Translating the science of good nutrition into the art of delectable meals."

Wendy Gauthier gets publicity for the cakes and treats she makes for dogs and uses this to make people familiar with the people-food side of her business. Vicki Brown gets referrals from doctors for patients on strict diets. Senior citizens make up a large part of her clientele. Randy Eckstein has a medical and biology background (which makes him very comfortable working with patients on medically restricted diets) and is experienced in cooking without wheat, soy, or corn.

Pauline Reep's culinary business began as a cake-decorating business. She usually makes her clients something special on their birthdays. "After they realize I can provide this service, they usually start ordering special desserts and give my name out to others."

- Much of your research can become information for your website. The Web is the fastest and easiest way to grow any business. Peruse as many food or personal chef websites as you can, and see how they sell themselves. Are pictures of luscious food effective? Can you snap a few professional-looking pictures with your digital camera? Could you photograph your own beautiful holiday table as an example of your work? Think of your website as a letter to a friend who you want to fill in on all your good news. Chapter 6 includes suggestions and ideas about developing a website for your business.

Step 9: Crunching the Numbers

- Being realistic about the numbers is your only chance of long-term success in any business. Start simply. You have to know how much money it takes for you to live each month. With computers, accounting software, and good advice from a friendly accountant, budgets and finances are easy to create and understand.
- Do you have good accounting practices already? Is your checkbook balanced and accurate? Your business accounts are going to have to be. Don't let these business questions scare you. It's harder to make a perfect meal than it is to balance a budget. The easiest place to start is a personal income and expense statement. Simply take a piece of paper and write how much you take in or make each month at the top of the page. Underneath that, list every single expense you have. Are you solvent already? Do you save money each month or are you just getting by? If you quit your job, what other benefits besides income will you lose? Can you afford to start a new business?
- Can you figure out a way to work part-time at your old job and still start your new business? Work smart.
- If you have a partner or family, they need to express their feelings about you starting a new business. You owe it to them. Open communications will help solve problems.

Step 10: Applying For a Loan

You may decide to take a loan in order to start your business. This is an important decision and it will benefit you greatly to make that decision an educated one. Some initial steps include getting clarity on how much you need to borrow, and making a budget for your business so it will be clear to the prospective lender (and to you) where the money will go.

Be a good loan shopper! Remember that there are many types of loans: short-term, long-term, variable, fixed, etc. Do some research and take your time to read the fine print on each loan, as annoying as that can be.

Once you have found a loan that feels like a good fit, the next step is to create a loan proposal. If you have a business plan, you are more than halfway there!

Here is what to include in your loan proposal:

- Your company name
- What your company does (explain clearly, as many folks don't quite understand the term "personal chef")
- The amount of the loan
- How you plan to use the money
- When and how you intend to pay back the loan
- Your financial projection for the next year
- Your credit report (www.freecreditreport.com)
- Your business plan

Submitting a loan proposal is an instance where more is better. Use of charts, especially for your financial projections and your plans for the money borrowed, is very helpful. The goal is to present a clear outline of your wonderful business.

04 The Legal Side of Food Preparation

Every business owner will make mistakes. The purpose of this chapter is to keep you from making mistakes that could cost you your business or your good reputation. In this chapter we'll discuss what you need to know about city ordinances, health department regulations, and insurance needs; where you can and can't cook; how to protect yourself and your clients with written agreements; and keeping accurate records in case you-know-what does hit the fan.

What You Need to Know about City Ordinances

Although it may be tempting to skip the paperwork and just start cooking, it is important to establish your personal chef business as just that—a business. One of the first things to do is to call or visit your local city clerk's office and find out exactly what rules you need to follow in your community. Rules, ordinances, and requirements change from city to city and state to state. As you call around, you might very well get three different answers to the same question. This is never reassuring. Take notes, names, and numbers and just persevere. If you are ever questioned about anything, at least you will be able to say who told you what when.

When I call the city or the health department, I often ask if whomever I am speaking with can send me copies of the documents they are referring to or reading from. They can mail, fax, or e-mail me, or I offer to pick the papers up. You might need this information to get insurance, for tax issues or planning, or for explaining to your clients why you must do things in a certain way.

Can You Have a Home Office?

Can you legally use your home address for your business office? There are many cities in the United States that will not allow any kind of business, even just an office, in a private home. Of course you will be using your home to do your paperwork and so forth; the issue is whether you can use it as a deduction. Using a home office as a tax deduction will be something you need to check out.

What Address Should You Use?

Do you want to use your home address, or would it be better to have a post office box for business mail and payment delivery? Obviously, it's cheaper to use your home address, but if you have several people in your house who get lots of mail, your business mail could get lost in the shuffle. Taking your home address out of the loop might be the way to go. A small post office box will cost you between $16 and $40 a month.

Do You Need a Business License?

Depending on where you live, you may or may not need a business license. In Los Angeles, the moment you become a vendor to another business (this could happen if a client pays you through their business or with a business check rather than with a personal check), your name will pop up on a business list, and the city or cities involved will track you down and request your business license. Why? Because this is how cities make their revenue.

I know of several personal chefs that live in cities and states that do not require them to have a business license. When I first started out, my business license only cost me $100. Now it exceeds $1,500 yearly. It is based on a percentage of my yearly gross sales. My accountant takes care of the paperwork for me for $30, and I just sign the check.

Once you find out if you can legally operate your office out of your home, inquire about a business license from your city clerk's office. If your city doesn't require it, you may want to get one anyway. Without a business license you may not be able to get business liability insurance or a federal tax ID number, which you need if you want to open a business bank account.

Do You Need A DBA? What The Heck Is A DBA?

DBA stands for "Doing Business As." It is basically a form you fill out that will secure that your business name is protected (and to make sure you are not using a business name that is already in use).

There are many benefits of having a DBA. It separates your legal name from your business should your business not work out. It will allow you to open a business checking account with your company name if you are a sole proprietor. And it creates legitimacy for your service and your brand.

DBA rules and requirements vary from state to state (for example, some states do not require that your business name be original and you can share a business name with someone else). Googling DBA requirements with the name of your county and state should provide you with a wealth of information.

Do You Need a Business Bank Account?

Again, this is about running a business. Do you want to just operate out of your personal checking account and use your social security number as identification? I think that's fine if you're the only person using that checking account. But if you are married or living with a partner that has access to your checking account, I would definitely want my business account separate. It's clearer and cleaner. And when it's time to pay taxes, you have your checkbook as a record of your business income and expenses.

Personally, I hate accounting, but I learned that if I did a little bit every day and kept accurate records in my accounting software, I was aware of each penny I had and every penny I spent. And slowly but surely I learned to manage my money better. It's simple math. Know how much you spend, how much you take in, and what your profit is for each and every cook date.

Do You Need an Employee Identification Number?

An Employee Identification Number (EIN) is a federal tax ID number that is given to you by the IRS.

You DO NOT need to obtain an EIN if:

- You are a sole proprietor
- You have no employees
- You do not collect excise taxes

You DO need to obtain an EIN if:

- You have an LLC or a corporation
- You file pensions
- You have employees

Visit www.IRS.gov and select "businesses" from the horizontal bar at the top of the home page. The website will explain more and provide the forms you need to get started.

Do You Need to Charge Sales Tax?

Many cities require caterers to charge sales tax on their food and their service. Some only need to charge tax on their service fee. Providing a service is taxable in the city of Los Angeles. The state of Washington requires personal chefs, or chefs for hire, to charge sales tax. All this is very confusing. I wish I could give you a "yes" or "no" answer, but every city handles this issue differently. You will need to check this with your local tax board.

Sales tax can have a huge impact on your business, so find this out before you start billing your clients. Some localities include personal chef services under the umbrella of catering, and all the rules, regulations, and taxes that apply to catering also apply to them. If you haven't collected sales tax and the tax board in your area decides you should have, you have no recourse. The tax board will most likely fine you and demand payment on all previous PC income. They could audit you (and charge you for the audit), fine you, and possibly charge you a late fee. It's not pretty, and there is no way to recoup that money. Can you imagine calling up clients you cooked for months ago and asking them for sales tax now? Why am I seeing a snowball in hell?

When researching tax laws across the country as they pertain to personal chef businesses, it became clear to me that this is an industry that is still evolving. When cities realize they're losing possible income, personal chefs will be paying more taxes.

A personal chef with a business in Wisconsin was told no taxes were necessary on her service fee and no taxes needed to be charged on groceries for which she was reimbursed. But she kept her payments separate regardless: one invoice for her service and another for the groceries. This was an excellent instinct on her part because later on, her tax board told her that if the two invoices were combined she would have to apply sales tax to the total because she was selling prepared meals. Does this make sense to you? It doesn't to me. Carefully research sales tax in your area.

My prediction for the future is that because cities, states, and the government are always broke, they will decide that the 10,000 or more personal chefs working across the country could supply a tidy sum in taxes.

Obtaining a Safe Food Handler's Certification

If you did not receive a safe food handler's certification through school or other culinary training, you may want to consider getting one when starting your business. It may not necessarily be a legal requirement in your state, but regardless it is a great way to ensure the safety of your clients and the reputation of your service. There are many online avenues that will help you complete your certification. What this usually entails is first completing an online course. This course will quiz you on your knowledge as you progress. Once you have completed the course, you will schedule a time to take an in-person examination that, once passed, will earn you your certification.

When a personal chef friend of mine went through this recently, she got confused because she thought the whole process would take place online. When it was time to take the exam, she was given a list of local certified instructors (or "proctors") who would administer the exam either in the comfort of her home or at their office location. She then learned that she could have bypassed the entire online course and received training *and* the exam in one day from this instructor.

The moral of the story? Figure out what works best for you. Had my friend known that she would eventually have to take an in-person exam, she would have opted to receive the training from that same person.

We recommend that you go to www.ServSafe.com and click on "Find a Proctor." You should find a list of certified proctors you can contact to price their cost for training and certification (we found that the prices did vary a bit, so go with the person from whom you get the best vibe).

Once certified, you are good for the next five years. Nice!

How Your Local Health Department Affects Your Business

Different localities have different regulations pertaining to personal chef services and where and how they can cook. No localities that I am aware of allow you to prepare food any place other than the home of your client. Under no circumstances are you allowed to make food in one location and deliver it to another location. If you do that, you are considered a caterer, and you need to prepare the food in a health department–permitted kitchen.

As a personal chef (or, as some states will refer to you, as a chef for hire) you are required to cook all the food in your client's home using their major appliances. You can bring some pots and pans, but leave your stove at home.

The difference between providing a service and providing a product is a particularly important one where the health department is concerned. If you prepare food off-site and deliver it to a client, you are either a caterer or a restaurant with take-out service. Any caterer's or restaurant kitchen is required to be an inspected and permitted kitchen. Those permits are a yearly expense for these businesses, the cost of which is based on the square footage of their kitchens. The bigger the kitchen, the more it costs for the permit. The requirements and codes for these kitchens cost the owners quite a bit of money in building and upkeep.

As a personal chef, the kitchen you work in is supplied to you free of charge because it belongs to your client. It's up to you to make sure your food is safe and sanitary. And your client is counting on that.

Your local health department can provide you with valuable information on food safety, from sourcing to proper cooking to storage. It makes good business sense to stay on top of the latest information. You want to be confident that you are serving your clients the safest food possible, and your clients want to be confident in your knowledge, professionalism, and dedication. Call your local health department and find out what regulations pertain to you. See page 7 for a list of excellent reading on food safety.

Cooking in Your Clients' Kitchens

Cooking in your clients' kitchens not only makes sense and, from a legal standpoint, is required, it can also save you time. You won't have to worry about the logistics of safely transporting and storing cooked food. Additionally, preparing food in your clients' kitchens, cooling it properly, and storing it in their refrigerator and freezer ensures that your clients are always getting the safest and freshest meals possible.

Cooking for Your Clients in Your Kitchen

The only way you can use your own kitchen to prepare food that you sell to other people is to have a kitchen that is approved by your local health department. This isn't going to happen unless your kitchen is built to code and outfitted as a commercial kitchen. And wherever it sits must be legally allowed under the zoning regulations. In Salt Lake City, Utah, on the same property that your home is on, or in the basement or garage of your home, you are allowed to build a separate commercial kitchen, but it cannot have any direct access to the personal areas of your home. And it must be considered a legal business under the existing zoning laws in that area.

Once again, this is an area in which all localities differ in their requirements. Food for sale to the public must be protected.

If your business grows or you want to expand, the most likely scenario is to rent professional kitchen space from a caterer, bakery, or restaurant that has downtime you can take advantage of. Get your own health department permit, and make the most of the rental time. In doing so you may be considered under the law as a caterer along with being a personal chef. This means that you may have to get an additional license and follow other local regulations. You will also want to make sure your liability insurance covers you when using this new location. Simply renting space from an existing caterer does not mean that it's a legal, sanctioned kitchen with the proper permits.

When You Need an Attorney

An attorney can be helpful if you are setting up your business as a partnership with another personal chef. Do you need a partnership agreement? Can you write a partnership agreement yourself? Sure you can. There are many books dedicated to this very subject. Most important to any partnership agreement are the paragraphs that explain how partners end their partnership. Oh my, just like love, it's so much easier getting married than it is getting divorced.

If you are going into a partnership, I suggest you list all your assets going in. Talk honestly about what potential problems there could possibly be. Make sure the division of labor is set down in writing. Never assume anyone has the same ideas or values as you. Ignoring these things or thinking that everything will take care of itself is a setup for failure.

Another subject to discuss with an attorney is what potential problems could arise while you are in a client's home. What happens if you are injured or you break something of theirs that cannot be replaced? What do you do if your client gets sick from something you made? And what if this causes them to miss the most important business meeting of their life? If you know what the probable outcome is, you will better know how to protect yourself beforehand. It's the "Tell me the worst thing that can happen to me" approach to planning.

Insurance: Protecting Yourself and Your Clients

Liability insurance is offered through membership in organizations like the United States Personal Chef Association. Packages are customized for personal chefs and could be your best value, but it depends on your assets, your business goals, and your personal finances to determine if these packages offer enough coverage or are comprehensive enough for you.

Because personal cheffing is such a new business, most insurance companies will have no idea how to handle your needs. Plan for confusion, and be ready to explain exactly *why* you are not a caterer. With that said, let me give you an overview of small business insurance so you'll know what to ask for and what to discuss. Also talk to your independent insurance agent, who will be able to help navigate what and how much insurance you will need.

Larger companies like State Farm offer customized packages designed for home businesses. You might find their website informative: www.statefarm.com.

Types of Coverage

- *Property Insurance.* Beyond just your homeowners or rental property insurance. Make sure your insurance agent is aware of your office equipment and any other equipment that you use for your business.
- *Personal Liability Umbrella.* What happens if you damage something that belongs to your client? Will this policy stretch to cover product liability? What if something you serve your client makes them sick? What if they have to visit a doctor or emergency room?
- *Loss of Income/Disability Income.* What happens if you get hurt and can't work? How do you pay your bills?

Bonding

If you have employees that work directly with your clients, a client may ask you if the employee is bonded. Bonds are also called theft bonds, surety bonds, or fidelity bonds, and they basically protect the client should the client's employee be convicted of theft.

Bonds are not normally required by a business owner who has general liability insurance, as most liability insurance covers this risk. However, if you have employees, it is something worth looking into as bonds are not expensive (usually a few hundred dollars per year), and may give you and your clients ease and confidence that you are fully covered.

Written Agreements

A written contract may seem unnecessary, but writing details down will nip most problems in the bud, because most problems that arise are the result of miscommunication. You don't have to call it a contract or an agreement if you don't want to, but you should create some sort of written memo stating what services you are providing; defining equipment, shopping, and transportation; and specifying what your cancellation policy is. Add what your services cost, what the client's inclusive costs will be, and when payment is expected.

Take a look at the sample client worksheet on page 54. Not only does it keep track of everything you need to remember but, along with a client questionnaire (pages 58–59), it gives you a script for selling your services and closing deals.

If you've had a few conversations with a prospective client, write the information you've gathered in the appropriate spaces on the client worksheet. When you next speak to your client, you can fill in the rest. The more information you have, the better the service you will provide. And by demonstrating your business skills to your client right from the beginning, you are inspiring trust in your professionalism.

When the You-Know-What Hits the Fan

Keeping track of every communication you have with clients will help you to reconstruct events if something goes awry. Notes from conversations, copies of e-mails, anything that has to do with your client should all go in a client folder. This is a private place; no one will see this but you. Write what you know, feel, and experience. In the initial meeting, is the prospective client telling you he hates strangers in his home? Does he say he hired this "stupid girl last year who made awful food and didn't clean up after herself?"

There are better ways to say the last personal chef experience didn't live up to expectations. Consider whether this would be a good client to take on. He is already annoyed. Is he going to think you are perfect in comparison? Or will you be looking down the barrel of a shotgun?

My husband is an attorney, and when I tell him stories like this, he tells me that the client has just told you exactly what he's like. You decide if this client is worth your time and trouble. Trust your gut instinct.

When something does go very wrong, try to remain calm. Try seeing things from your client's point of view. Did the dog get out because you left the gate unlatched?

Client name: _____

Names of other family members you will be cooking for: _____

Ages of children: _____

Address: _____

City, state, ZIP: _____

Cell, home, and work phone numbers: _____

E-mail address: _____

Emergency contact name and number: _____

Date of start of service: _____

Number of servings per meal: _____

Date and time when cooking in client's kitchen: _____

Frequency of service (once a week, every other week, once a month, etc.): _____

Description of how you will leave their meals (in disposables, in their containers, etc.): _____

_____

Description of what they are to provide (freezer space, whatever else you need from them): _____

_____

Cost breakdown: Service fee: _____

                      Groceries billed separately: _____

                      Deposit required: _____

                      Balance due: _____

                      Date balance due: _____

Special requests or additions that require additional cost: _____

Allergies or health concerns: _____

Kitchen quirks: _____

Entering and exiting instructions: _____

Alarm: _____

Fuse/breaker box: _____

Pets: _____

Other: _____

Date: _____

Client name: _____

Address: _____

City, state, ZIP: _____

Home phone: _____

Work phone: _____

Cell phone: _____

E-mail address: _____

Day and time you will be cooking in your client's home: _____

_____

Frequency of service (once a week, every other week, once a month, etc.): _____

_____

Number of servings: _____

Client to supply containers or I supply disposables at additional cost? _____

Description of what they are to provide (freezer space, whatever else you need from them):

_____

_____

Balance due: _____

Date balance due: _____

Cancellation and refund policy: * _____

_____

All deposits are nonrefundable.

* Explain here about your cancellation policy. For example, I would request at least three days' notice
to change a cook date. A minimal fee might be charged to change the date. If your clients know
there is a penalty, they are less apt to cancel or make changes. If I show up at my client's home
with groceries and my client has left town with no word to me, I bill for the groceries and for my
service fee. If they want our relationship to continue, they will need to pay me. Be aware that you
must tell your clients up front what your cancellation and refund policy are. This is a two-way
street. If you cancel on them, how do you make it up to them?

Did you break her favorite crystal vase? Did you throw out the last of her Beluga caviar without asking, even though it was moldy and starting its own ecosystem?

Anything and everything can go wrong. How it affects your business depends on how you choose to respond to it. I've cooked for some of the richest people in the world. At one place there was a Picasso hanging above the stove. I am not making this up. This did not inspire me to cook. It made me a nervous wreck. I asked them to remove it; they didn't understand why I was nervous! I mean, it wasn't like it was the Renoir or anything! Silly me.

I've found the best communication strategy is to be straightforward with my clients. In return, I hope they will be the same with me.

What to Cook and How to Charge for It

The second most common problem for the new personal chef—right behind undercharging clients—is making either too much or too little food. This can be as deadly to your business as underpricing your menus. In this chapter I will tell you how to accurately estimate how much food to make for your clients and how much you should charge for it.

Portion sizes vary in recipes, in clients' minds, in cookbooks, and in the government food pyramid. I have never gotten 100 chocolate chip cookies out of a bag of Nestlé chocolate chips. And yet the recipe always tells me that the yield is 100 cookies. It's best for you to calculate portion sizes and educate your client what to expect early in your relationship.

Getting to know your clients is the key to knowing how to cook the best food for their particular needs. Sitting down with them and going over the client questionnaire on pages 58–59 is an excellent place to start.

How to Estimate the Right Food Quantities

There are various factors that come into play when deciding the amount of food you need to allow for each person. For years I have managed to make just the right amount of food for every client by taking into account the following factors.

The Ages of Your Clients

The older your clients are, the less they tend to eat. Envision the amount of food that a family with athletic teenagers eats for dinner compared with the amount that a retired couple with sedentary lifestyles might consume. You also might want to read up on aging taste buds and using salt substitutes (the AARP's website has some useful information: www.AARP.org). Unfortunately,

Client Questionnaire

1. Do you have any food allergies or sensitivities that you are aware of? How about the rest of your family?
2. Do you have any health concerns or conditions that affect your diet?
3. Would you like your meals prepared following a particular diet? Do you have a cookbook you could share with me, or a recommendation on one I should purchase?
4. Do you like hearty portions, or do you want your portion size controlled? When I cook, I typically plan for 4 ounces of protein, 3 ounces of a vegetable side, and 3 ounces of carbohydrate/starch.
5. What are some of your favorite foods?
6. What foods do you dislike? What about the rest of your family?
7. Are you physically active? What kind of exercise do you do on a regular basis?
8. Which matters to you more: taste or health?
9. What's the single most important thing you'd like to get out of my personal chef service?
10. What expectations do you have of our relationship and my services?
11. How do you want your meals packaged—individual servings or family servings?
12. Do you prefer fine dining or everyday food?
13. Do you have specific cuisines that you favor over others?
14. Shall I discuss the menus with you ahead of time, or is it up to me to choose the menus? I can e-mail selections once a month for you to choose.
15. What days are best for me to prepare your food in your kitchen?
16. Do you want the standard 5x4 service? This is five different meals of four servings each, three days of meals left refrigerated and the rest frozen.
17. Or would you like the standard fresh service (6x4 service divided into two separate cook dates), which leaves you with only refrigerated foods and nothing frozen? With this service, I can cook for you once a week for two weeks or twice in one week. This service costs more than the standard 5x4 service.
18. How often do you want my services: weekly, twice monthly, once a month?
19. Do you want the basic meal consisting of protein, vegetable, and starch?

20. Would you like to add an appetizer, salad, or soup to your meal at an additional cost?

21. Would you like dessert included with your meals at an additional cost?

22. Generally, I will leave two or three meals in your refrigerator and freeze the rest with reheating instructions attached. Will this work for you?

23. Do you favor salt or like saltier foods? Or are you trying to cut down on salt?

24. Are you sensitive to spicy foods?

25. Do you prefer organic products even though this will increase the cost of your meals?

26. Are there certain flavors or textures that you don't like?

27. Do you like meats cooked rare, medium, or well done?

28. If this is part of a weight loss or health goal, do you have a period of time in which you would like to achieve this goal?

29. How would you like your meals packaged? Will you supply reusable plastic? Would you prefer I buy disposables? Or will aluminum pans work for you?

30. Would you consider using my services to cook for dinner parties, special occasions, or holidays?

31. Is there anything else you would like to tell me about yourself and food?

32. Would you prefer that I contact you with questions via phone or e-mail?

taste buds diminish as we age. Along with health restrictions, it can make for challenges in cooking. Can you add more salt or spice? Or do high blood pressure and ulcers preclude that?

The Lifestyle of Your Clients

Are your clients single or married? Do they have a healthy lifestyle or are they used to fast food? Do they follow diet trends or just enjoy basic, tasty foods? An active couple is going to eat more than a single, sedentary client. A client who leads a very healthy lifestyle and is a calorie counter is going to eat significantly less than a client who doesn't really care about the fat and calories in the food just as long as it tastes good. Do your clients drink wine with dinner? Do they have a cocktail when they get home from work? All this can influence selections, taste, and portion sizes.

The Health Concerns of Your Clients

Are your clients trying to lose weight? Have they hired you in an attempt to eat healthier? Are they on a restricted diet? The type of food you cook will have an impact on the food cost and on the time it takes you to produce it. Special diets that are unfamiliar to you will take you longer to prepare than food that is in your personal cooking comfort zone.

You must make allowances for the extra time and effort it will take you to plan menus for a client with dietary needs that are unfamiliar to you. If you keep track of your time, you will find that special requests are costing you more money in planning and possibly in shopping and groceries. You'll need to adjust your fees as you gain experience and begin to realize how much time it takes you to handle special diets. Of course, once you know a particular diet backward and forward, you can charge less for it. Or simply reap more profit.

Los Angeles–based chef Jeff Parker shared with me his interview process with new clients. His client interview form is on pages 61-63.

From Planning to Cooking

It is important that you know how long you will spend menu planning, shopping, schlepping, cooking, packaging, labeling, and cleaning up so that you can charge enough to make this venture worth your time. You will be buying plastic wrap and garbage bags, salt and pepper, labels, envelopes, and postage. You will also be spending time communicating with your clients to fine-tune their menus, billing your clients, putting gas in your car, packing your kits, maintaining your equipment, and many other odds and ends that will take more time than you may realize. After twenty-five years of cooking, I know this: Everything takes longer than you think it will.

All these tasks add up. You need to keep track of all your time and all your expenses and factor these into your total service fee. Otherwise you are giving your time away for free, and that is no way to run a business or make enough money to support yourself. Imagine your business five years out. Will you have made enough to stay with it? You don't want to just break even or constantly be hoping for the next year to be better. Trust me, you're going to get tired of the struggle. A passion for cooking is not enough.

Do you enjoy soups as a main entree? ☐ YES ☐ NO ☐ HOT ☐ COLD
Do you enjoy salads as a main entree? ☐ YES ☐ NO ☐ HOT ☐ COLD
Do you enjoy pastas as an entree? ☐ YES ☐ NO ☐ HOT ☐ COLD

How many times per month do you enjoy the following?
Beef:_____ Pork:_____ Turkey:_____ Fish:_____
Chicken:_____ ☐ White ☐ Dark ☐ On-bone ☐ Off-bone
Fish types: _____
Shellfish types:_____

Do you enjoy vegetarian entrees? ☐ YES ☐ NO ☐ SOMETIMES
Do you enjoy:
　☐ Grains ☐ Beans ☐ Bulgur ☐ Nuts ☐ Cheese ☐ Soy cheese

Favorite cheeses: _____
Are you lactose intolerant? ☐ YES ☐ NO
Are you allergic to anything? ☐ YES ☐ NO
Do you have any other food sensitivities? ☐ YES ☐ NO
If yes, please list: _____

Are there any fruits or vegetables that you particularly like or dislike?
Likes: _____
Dislikes: _____

Are there other flavors that you particularly dislike? ☐ YES ☐ NO
If yes, please list: _____

May I cook with alcohol?   ☐ YES   ☐ NO

Do you have any of the following conditions?

     ☐ Diabetes   ☐ Heart problems

     ☐ High blood pressure requiring: ☐ Light salt   ☐ No salt

     ☐ High cholesterol requiring: ☐ Low fat   ☐ No fat

Are you trying to lose weight?   ☐ YES   ☐ NO

Would you like portion control?   ☐ YES   ☐ NO

Are you on a particular diet?   ☐ YES   ☐ NO

If yes, which one? _____

Do you particularly like or dislike any of the following cuisines?

☐ Mexican/Latin	☐ LIKE	☐ DISLIKE
☐ Thai	☐ LIKE	☐ DISLIKE
☐ Chinese	☐ LIKE	☐ DISLIKE
☐ Japanese	☐ LIKE	☐ DISLIKE
☐ French	☐ LIKE	☐ DISLIKE
☐ Italian	☐ LIKE	☐ DISLIKE
☐ Other: _____		

Indicate the level of spiciness you prefer:

     ☐ Bland   ☐ Mild   ☐ Medium   ☐ Hot   ☐ Laser   ☐ Incredibly painful

Do you want breads, rolls, or tortillas as part of your meals?   ☐ YES   ☐ NO

If yes, please list your favorites: whole wheat or white or something else:

_____

Do you like salads with your entrees?   ☐ YES   ☐ NO

Please list favorite salad greens: _____

Do you like cherry tomatoes?   ☐ YES   ☐ NO

Do you have favorite recipes you would like me to use?　□ YES　　□ NO
If yes, please list or provide: _____

How would you prefer to have your meals packaged?
       □ Individually　　□ For two　　□ Family style

Would you prefer semidisposables or reusables?
       □ Semidisposable (Gladware) $15 per visit charge
       □ Reusable (Pyrex or Corningware) $100 deposit required

About your appliances:
Stove:	□ Gas	□ Electric	Do all burners function?	□ YES	□ NO
Oven:	□ Gas	□ Electric	Functioning and accurate?	□ YES	□ NO
Does your microwave work?				□ YES	□ NO
Does your garbage disposable work?				□ YES	□ NO
Do you have an additional freezer?				□ YES	□ NO

Location:_____

How will you most likely reheat your entrees?　　□ Oven　　□ Microwave

Is there anything else I should be made aware of?

_____
_____
_____
_____
_____
_____
_____
_____
_____

Accounting for the Personal Chef

Later in this chapter I will show you how to figure out what your expenses are and describe the different ways you can charge for your services. But first I want to discuss basic accounting and what it has to do with your business. Many a talented small businessperson has failed because of inept bookkeeping. If you don't know how much money is coming in and going out, you don't have a chance of success.

There are all kinds of software systems to help you stay organized (see appendix F for a short list). It's not difficult; it's all about being accurate and not falling behind. There are three basic principles to keep in mind for personal chef accounting:

1. Invoicing
2. Income
3. Expenses

Basic accounting shouldn't take very much of your time. Invoicing your clients and keeping track of your income, then deducting your expenses, is really all you need to do. Take all your income, subtract your expenses, and what's left is your profit. If you keep up to date, when tax time rolls around, you'll have all the necessary information in one place.

Cash Flow

Cash flow is an important concept to grasp. Simply put, cash is money you can get your hands on immediately. This does not include any other assets that you own (house, car, equipment, etc.).

In your business, your *cash output* goes to the following:

- Expenses
- Employees
- Taxes

Conversely, *cash input* comes from your clients. The goal is to have positive cash flow; more cash comes in than goes out. When you are beginning your business, having greater output is common due to various investments including marketing costs, building up your kit to take to clients' homes, or offering free or reduced service to establish your name in the community. This time of heavy cash output should be clearly planned for.

Here are a few terms you are likely to hear about finances. When I started, much of this was foreign to me, and it's less scary to navigate the financial waters if you know what the heck everybody is talking about. I want you to feel empowered as a new business owner!

- Cash Flow Projection: These are reports that predict what the future of your business will look like. There are short-term (less than one year), and long-term (three to five years) projections. These reports are like a skeleton for your business. If you know what the numbers are likely to be, you can plan your growth accordingly. I've also found it helpful in goal setting ("Wow! If I get four weekly clients for $300 a day each, I can take the month of August off!").

- Sales Revenue or Gross Income: This is your total income for the business. Most people do an annual tally of their total sales.
- Operating Cash Flow or Net Income: This is the money you make minus all of the expenses it takes to run your business.

How to Invoice

I discuss how to figure out what to charge for your services later in this chapter. If you have an accounting program like Microsoft Money Small Business or Quicken Premier Home & Business, you can automatically generate custom invoices. This section has a basic invoice form that you can use, or design your own based on this information.

Basic Expenses

Many people do not realize how much time and money it takes to run a business—even a one-person personal chef business. The only way to do this is to *write it all down*. After you figure out your expenses, then you can go on to the next step of figuring out which pricing system is best for you.

Use a calculator and fill out the basic expense chart on page 68. Some of these expenses occur weekly or monthly, whereas others may only happen yearly. Don't forget anything! You can keep track of your entire year of expenses on a spreadsheet in your computer. If you know how to use Excel, you can customize it for your own business. QuickBooks or Quicken are also fine programs to help you keep track. You want to know how much you have to spend to run your business each month so that you won't undersell your services.

When you work as a food consultant for a client, you need to charge them for your time. Think of it this way: They are saving money they would have otherwise spent at Weight Watchers or Jenny Craig.

Let me give you an example: You spend two to three hours planning, researching, and developing low-fat menus for a client, plus an hour of bookkeeping for this client each week, but you are only billing them for one cook date. How will you repay yourself those additional hours? 4 hours x 4 weeks = 16 hours a month. If you are making about $20 an hour for the average cook date, then you are losing $320 on that client each month.

Jennifer's
Personal Chef Service

Invoice

March 1, 2010

Los Angeles, CA 90035

310-555-1234

Fed Tax ID: 12-3456789

Bill to: Jackie and Tony Meyer

Address: 1234 Happy Home Street

Los Angeles, CA 90035

Phone: 310-555-4321

DESCRIPTION	AMOUNT
Personal Chef Services Standard 5x4	$350.00
Groceries	$157.93
Minus deposit	−$150.00
TOTAL	$357.93

Please make all checks payable to Jennifer Story. Balance due within ten days.

Thank you for your business!

Basic Overhead Expense Form

	January	February	March	1st Quarter Total
EXPENSES				
Gas				
Other auto (repair, insurance)				
Business books and cookbooks				
Magazines				
Uniform purchase and cleaning				
Equipment purchase: knives, pots and pans, kit boxes, etc.				
Pantry items and supplies				
Equipment repair and knife sharpening				
Office supplies: business cards, mailings, flyers, etc.				
Phone/cell service				
Internet service				
Insurance/license fees				
Advertising/Web site costs				
Membership fees				
Accounting fees				
Total expenses				

2011 expenses

JANUARY

DEDUCTIBLE BUSINESS EXPENSES

DATE	DESCRIPTION	FOOD restaurants grocery	SUPPLIES equipment, computer, office, work clothes	UTILITIES 100% Internet, cell/home phone	UTILITIES PARTIAL rent, water, power, gas	AUTO insurance, repairs, gas, parking, fees	TRAVEL transport, lodging, baggage, fees, supplies	RESEARCH magazine, books, etc.	MEME-BERSHIPS meetings, expense, books	FEES bank account service fees	NON-DEDUCTIBLE EXPENSES
Total by category											
Percentage deductible		100%	100%	100%	20%	75%	100%	100%	100%	100%	0%
Total amount deductible											

JANUARY TOTAL AMOUNT DEDUCTIBLE

What if you have four clients that you're spending this time on? $320 x 4 = $1,280. Get my drift?

Determining Your Profit

Now that you know your expenses, let's take a look at how you can maximize your profit. Personal chefs generally bill per hour, per meal, or per day. They sometimes sell a package of meals per week or month. Hourly fees vary based on location (you may be able to charge more if you live in New York than if you live in Des Moines), and your profits depend on how many jobs you are able to take on, how fast you cook, how well you sell, and realistic pricing.

Let me give you some examples: A standard day in the culinary world is ten hours. In doing a bit of research, I found that most personal chefs charge between $200 and $350 per day.

In a high-priced market like New York, Los Angeles, or San Francisco, experienced personal chefs are able to earn as much as $400 a day, sometimes more. If you live in a smaller market, you may only be able to charge $225 a day, but the cost of living is probably less, so it all evens out. (When you feel badly about your hourly wage, consider all your culinary brethren who are slaving away for barely minimum wage in restaurants all over town.)

How to Price Your Menus

Because most personal chefs start their business the day they get their very first job, they do not have the experience to know how much it all costs or how long it takes to make the menus their clients have requested. The more clients you get and jobs you do, the more accurately you will be able to price your menus. You'll also produce food faster and more efficiently. Time is your earning power, so it is a must to learn time management and how to charge for it accordingly.

Different personal chefs use different ways to calculate their service fees. The important thing is that you find one that fits your business that you feel comfortable with, and that takes your profit into account. You may find that you have to charge different fees to different clients. No one way is the only correct way. The following information will help you decide which way is best for you.

Simple Thirds

A basic starting point for setting fees is to divide your cook date fee in thirds: one third being the food cost, one third being your labor, and one third for your overhead and profit. Let's look at an example for a standard 5x4 service (five meals of four servings each, two to three left refrigerated and the remaining frozen) using this pricing formula. We are assuming a $250 service fee.

Divide **$250** into thirds = approximately **$83** per third.

Not to beat you over the head with it, but that's:

$83 food cost

$83 labor

$83 overhead expenses and profit

Can you make your client five dinners for $83 food cost? Maybe, if they only want rice and beans. Is $83 for your labor enough? Say your labor was ten hours; you've just made $8.30 an hour. How much job satisfaction does this give you? And the last third you've set aside for your overhead expenses (an average of $15 to $20 a cook date) and profit. Is $63 profit (before taxes) enough?

Even if you are scheduling five cook dates a week for $5,000 dollars a month in sales, you've pretty much hit the ceiling at $60,000 a year. That's $40,000 for your labor and profit. Less when you deduct your expenses.

Okay, now that I've depressed you, let's run the same exercise with a fee of $300 a cook date. Suddenly you have $100 for food cost, $100 for labor, and $100 for overhead and profit. Your ceiling just got higher: $72,000 a year. That's $48,000 for your labor and profit, less expenses.

Does your area, clientele, and skill make it possible to charge $300 a day for a cook date? Can you schedule five days a week? Can you physically work five days a week?

What I don't like about this fee structure is that it works until your food cost increases because of special requests from your clients, seasonality, and shortages. If they want leg of lamb instead of that lovely casserole, it's taking away from your profit.

Realize how valuable your service is when deciding and figuring out your fee. You may be a trained culinary professional or an extremely passionate and motivated home cook, eager to please and wanting to help others. Your talent is for hire. You are not domestic help that can be had at minimum wage. Value yourself and your services, and don't undersell yourself or your delicious food.

How to Make the Most of Your Groceries

Should you decide to charge clients a flat rate for your service, including groceries, there are a few things to consider.

YIELD

A food yield is the percentage of the food you actually use. For instance, you buy five pounds of potatoes, but by the time you peel them, chop them and cook them, you will have significantly less than five pounds. Any raw meat you purchase will lose significant yield through water loss while cooking.

The goal is to have high yield, which means the majority of your food costs translate into profit. An example of a product with high yield potential is a whole chicken: Boil whole, shred meat to use in multiple dishes, use the carcass to make broth to use in multiple dishes, and add organs to make a rich broth or gravy.

AS-PURCHASED COST

This is what you pay for at the store or from your supplier. Obviously you want to get the most out of your money and to create as many edible portions as possible.

EDIBLE PORTION COST

This is the cost of a single portion of food after it has been completely prepared. Let's say your client has requested sweet potato fries. You go to the store and are met with two options: buying whole, unpeeled sweet potatoes at $1 per pound, or buying washed, peeled, and cut sweet potatoes at $1.89 per pound.

While the as-purchased cost has an obvious winner (the unpeeled sweet potatoes), when you consider the yield will go down once you peel the potatoes as well as the time it will take to prep the potatoes for fries, it may be a better value for you and your business to go with the prepped potatoes.

If I am charging a client a flat rate for my service and the food, I try to weigh and measure what my menu is and how long it will take to cook and shop accordingly.

Fee Plus Groceries

Using this system, clients are charged your service fee plus the cost of their groceries (cost of containers are generally figured separately). It works like this: Before your cook date, you provide clients with an invoice of your service fee plus an estimate to go shopping for their groceries. The estimate for groceries is a deposit. Now you are using your client's money instead of your own, which is much smarter. You want to keep your business cash flow just that: flowing. If each week your various clients owe you hundreds of dollars for groceries, those are your receivables. Not only is it more of your cash tied up, but it's also more you have to collect.

So get the grocery (deposit) check before you go shopping. If they are established clients and you trust them, they can leave you the checks to pick up on your cook day. Before you leave their house, you leave them any change from the deposit (or an invoice for the difference, or just credit/debit them on the next invoice). Basically, your bookkeeping for this cook date is done. You can leave copies of the receipts, but you should keep the originals for your records. If these are established clients, you might want to invoice on a monthly basis rather than weekly. But ask yourself: Do you have enough cash flow to do that? Or do you need the weekly income?

When I was a personal chef, I had three weekly clients. I cooked at each of their homes once a week. To make billing easier, I had each household set up a charge at the local grocery and produce stores. I never had to handle product money. My clients and I had decided roughly what I thought I would spend each week, and that was it. I did tell them to send me a list of anything else they wanted at the beginning of the week or leave it for me, so I brought them additional items that they needed. I found this extra ten minutes of shopping to get their coffee and toilet paper created a world of good will, and they were billed by the stores. This system might come in handy in your area. No harm in trying.

I did find that fees vary widely across the country. In very small markets you might only be able to charge $250 for a standard 5x4 service. As a normal day will probably be about ten hours long, this means you are making $25 an hour, not counting any preparatory work you need to do for a client, like developing their menus or planning for special diets or paperwork time. This does not take into account any taxes or business fees that you need to pay or other related expenses. Suddenly, your $25 an hour is reduced to $20 or less, subtracting the big picture.

I'm sure the light is starting to go on, and you can see why getting faster in the kitchen affects your bottom line. Can you develop menus and dinner ideas that only require six hours of cooking? If you can, do it. Work toward efficiency. It's better to start high and come down if you find that the market won't support your fee.

Other parts of the country can support service fees of $400 or more. $350 is about average for most medium-size markets. A 5x4 service will generally cost $125 in groceries, maybe a little more or less depending on the specific menus, where you live, and the time of year. This is a gross oversimplification, but you need a number to work with when planning all this out.

All-Inclusive Service

Many personal chefs prefer to offer an all-inclusive service. This is one price that includes groceries and your fee. Because you control the food costs, you can control your profit. This works if you have a lot of input in what your clients eat. If they eat whatever you give them, then sell them your all-inclusive service. If they are very picky or have lots of specifications, this could end up eating into your profit. Prices generally come out to $10 to $20 per serving. The more servings you cook, the more profitable you become.

In an all-inclusive service, special diets, premium proteins, or organics will require a surcharge to make it profitable for you. You will not be using high-end proteins like lamb, veal, or prawns. If your clients have expensive tastes, you will want to steer them away from this type of service because they will not be happy with the meals they'll get.

One idea is to offer both types of services: fee plus groceries and all-inclusive. This way you can let clients choose what fits their needs best. Have sample menus from your all-inclusive service to show clients so they understand what they are getting. Once again, find out if your state requires you to charge sales tax, and figure and add that into your total.

Because of the ever-increasing cost of groceries, personal chef Betsy Rogers switched to a fee-plus-groceries pricing structure. Her service fee includes all her time plus the cost of packaging and pantry items (oils, vinegars, spices.). Here's how she breaks down her fee:

Two portions consisting of five entrees:
    $275 plus groceries
Four portions consisting of five entrees:
    $300 plus groceries

Six portions consisting of five entrees:

$325 plus groceries

Eight portions consisting of five entrees:

$350 plus groceries

Extra charge for special diets that take additional

menu planning

Reid Smith charges a fee of $360 plus tax for his standard 5x4 service, provided that travel time and dietary restrictions are within reason. An all-organic menu would result in an additional charge to cover the increased cost of the groceries.

Pauline Reep uses different formulas for different clients. Her weekly clients get charged hourly with a minimum number of hours, plus groceries. The majority of

Possible Business Deductions

Discuss with your accountant what products, supplies, and services you can deduct from your income. Below are just a few:

- Accounting fees

- Advertising costs

- Auto use and maintenance

- Conventions and trade shows

- Gifts to clients

- Home office expenses

- Insurance

- Interest on business loans

- Membership dues in professional organizations

- Chef clothing purchase and cleaning

- Travel expenses (as a food professional, part or all of your vacations may be considered business deductions)

	January	February	March	1st Quarter Total
INCOME				
Total PC service income	_____	_____	_____	_____
Other income	_____	_____	_____	_____
Reimbursements, if any	_____	_____	_____	_____
Total income:	_____	_____	_____	_____
EXPENSES				
Total overhead expenses from Basic Overhead Expense Form	_____	_____	_____	_____
Total cost of groceries	_____	_____	_____	_____
Total cost of disposables	_____	_____	_____	_____
Total expenses:	_____	_____	_____	_____

QUARTERLY PROFIT/LOSS

Deduct expenses from income to determine your profit or loss

	January	February	March	1st Quarter Total
Total income:	_____	_____	_____	_____
Total expenses:	_____	_____	_____	_____
Total profit/loss:	_____	_____	_____	_____

her clients get charged a base price of $350 for two people, plus $75 for each additional person, with an additional cost for special diets, long distances, organics or specialty items, and any extra sides or entrees. I like Pauline; she thinks like me.

Putting It All Together

Okay, now that you know your expenses and you are familiar with different ways to price your services, let's do a cost exercise. Fill in the chart on the next page. You won't know all the numbers, but I've given you enough information for you to make pretty good guesses.

Sample Menu Pricing Form

Below is an example of a menu pricing form. You can buy software that will figure all this out for you, but you should know how to do it with a pencil and a calculator anyway. You need to understand how it's done; this is a basic personal chef business skill.

MEAL 1

Description: Citrus Rosemary Chicken Breasts with Roasted Red Potatoes and Blue Lake Green Beans

4 servings

Ingredient purchase list:	Cost:
4 chicken breasts	13.99
Fresh rosemary	1.59
1 orange	0.38
1 lemon	0.29
2 limes	0.59
1 pound red potatoes	1.99
1 pound green beans	3.99
SUBTOTAL food costs for Meal 1:	22.82
Tax, if any:	—
TOTAL food costs for Meal 1:	**22.82**

Now divide **$22.82** by **4** servings to get to the cost of each serving: **$5.07.** For the sake of argument, say your other 4 meals that week cost about the same; this means that **$22.82 x 5 meals = $114.10.** If you've included your basic pantry items in your overhead expenses, you will not need to account for them here. You do, however, need to keep track of what you spend on disposables and how much you are reimbursed for them.

Client Cost Worksheet for a 5x4 Service

Service fee:	+ $300.00
Food cost:	− $114.10
Disposables cost:	− $17.50
Disposables reimbursement:	+ $20.00
	————
Profit before expenses:	+ $188.40
Adjusted overhead:	− $33.33
(see explanation below)	
	————
Total profit:	+ $155.07

If you filled out your basic overhead expense form on page 68, you will have a total amount for your overhead expenses for the quarter. We are now going to figure out your *adjusted overhead* and *total profit*. To make this explanation easier on both of us, I am going to assume a quarterly overhead expense total of **$1,200.**

Divide this amount by **3** months to find that your monthly operating expenses are **$400.** Best-case scenario: Assume you have cook dates **5** days a week with no work on the weekends. This means you are cooking **21** days a month. Divide **$400** by **21** to get your amount of daily overhead expenses: **$19.05.**

If you cook for **3** clients each week (or **12** clients a month), divide **$400** by **12** to get **$33.33.** Your service fee needs to be high enough to cover this amount or you will never come out ahead.

If you have only **6** clients a month, your overhead expenses will be twice that, or **$66.66.** As you can see, the fewer clients you have, the more you need to charge to cover your overhead expenses.

Pricing an All-Inclusive Service

If your service is all inclusive, then a rule of thumb is to assume $125 of your fee being spent directly on food cost (this is a general average for mid-market areas and non-organic products for 2010). This doesn't include your overhead expenses or disposables. Can you charge a sufficient fee for a 5x4 service to make this venture

Seasonality Chart for Fruits and Vegetables

Produce in season is more readily available, less expensive, and is usually better quality. Below is a general seasonality chart for you to refer to when planning your menus.

Winter	Spring	Summer	Fall
Avocados	Asparagus	Apricots	Apples
Broccoli	Avocados	Beans	Broccoli
Brussels sprouts	Beans	Beets	Brussels sprouts
Cabbage	Beets	Berries	Cabbage
Cauliflower	Berries	Cherries	Cauliflower
Celery root	Broccoli	Corn	Celery root
Fennel	Cabbage	Cucumbers	Cranberries
Grapefruit	Cucumbers	Dates	Cucumbers
Greens	Mangoes	Figs	Fennel
Mushrooms	Okra	Grapes	Greens
Oranges	Oranges	Mangoes	Mushrooms
Pears	Papayas	Melons	Oranges
Spinach	Peas	Peaches	Pears
Sweet potatoes	Peppers	Peppers	Persimmons
	Radishes	Plums	Pomegranates
	Spinach	Summer squash	Spinach
	Summer squash	Tomatoes	Sweet potatoes
	Turnips	Watermelon	Winter squash

worthwhile for you? Let's assume that it is your goal to walk away from a cook date with $200 profit (including your labor). Assuming that you handle the cost of disposables separately, you will need to charge:

+	$200.00	Target profit including labor
+	$125.00	Food cost
+	$33.33	Adjusted overhead
	—————	
=	$358.33	Total service fee required for $200 profit

This does not take into consideration any time you spend on planning menus or taking special diets into account. Is the $200 still a sufficient profit for you? Will your market support that service fee?

Food Costs and Your Menus

Don't guess on your food costs. It is not wise to assume you know how much product costs without verifying the prices. Many grocery stores have their prices listed online and so are easy to check. Prices on products change from season to season and even week to week. Do your calculations carefully, and recalculate until you get a number you can happily live with. If necessary, reprice your menus every six months. Your investment in time will definitely pay you back in dollars.

In order to control costs and make life easier in your kitchen, try selling menus you are familiar with whenever possible. As a personal chef, keep in mind that perfect menus are flavorful, colorful, nutritionally balanced, varied enough to appeal to a wide range of tastes, and in step with current food trends.

You may want to add a disclaimer to the bottom of your menus that reads: "All items and products subject to availability." You can also tell your clients that you will "take into account their preferences when making necessary substitutions."

Don't ever take the shortcut of pricing your menus according to your competition. It is not essential to have prices that match or beat your competition because prices don't tell you whether they're making any money. You want to compete, but you also want to make money and be profitable.

Try pricing out six to eight sample menus. With everything written down you can easily see where you can add value or cut costs. Document each dish with its own recipe card. For the long-term growth of your business and your reputation,

Cream of Broccoli Soup	Brand/Size	Price	Item $
2 tablespoons extra virgin olive oil	pantry item	--	--
2 cloves garlic, minced	1 head	.99/ea	.99
1/2 pound cauliflower	loose florets	3.49/lb	1.75
1 pound broccoli	loose crowns	1.99/lb	1.00
8 cups chicken stock	Imagine, 32 oz	4.39/ea	8.78
1/2 teaspoon salt	pantry item	--	--
2 teaspoons Dijon mustard	pantry item	--	--
1 tablespoon fresh tarragon	1 bunch, 0.5 oz	1.49/ea	1.49
Freshly ground black pepper	pantry item	--	--
Total price for recipe:			**$14.01**

Cream of Broccoli Soup

Method

1. Heat oil in a large pot over medium heat. Add garlic, and sauté for 1 minute. Add the cauliflower, broccoli, stock, and salt. Bring to a boil. Reduce heat and simmer until vegetables are tender, about 20 minutes. Stir in mustard and tarragon. Remove from heat and let cool slightly.
2. Working in batches, transfer into a blender or food processor, and process until smooth. Adjust seasoning, salt and pepper to taste. Thin with stock or water if too thick.

Notes: *For people who aren't on restricted diets, add 1/3 cup cream and 2 tablespoons unsalted butter to soup at the end for extra richness.*

it's important to be able to duplicate every recipe consistently to guarantee quality standards job after job. It is also a good idea to test your recipes first before putting them on a menu.

Fill out a recipe card with food costs like the sample on page 81 for one of your own recipes and see how much the food costs are for that single menu item. As you can see, pantry items that are already accounted for in overhead expenses are not billed separately. You may wish to charge something, like 10 or 20 cents for each pantry item, if you aren't keeping track of them in your expense worksheet.

If you have leftover product (a head of garlic as an example), you need to charge for the whole thing regardless. You might be tempted to leave it behind and use it on your next cook date, but there isn't any guarantee it will still be there.

Calculating Your Labor

Keep track of how long it takes you to grocery shop, cook, and package a meal for yourself. The more complicated the dish is to make, the higher the labor, and the higher the price you charge your client.

No matter if you are cooking a complete meal or a single dish, document on the recipe card or your menu pricing form how long it takes, the exact yield, and the level of expertise it takes to produce. If you discover that your labor costs are accumulating to greater than 15 percent of the menu price, you may want to consider raising your prices—or choose simpler recipes to make.

Estimated Shopping and Kitchen Prep Time

Number of servings:	Four
Time period:	One week: Five meals of four servings each
Menu type:	Upscale classic French
Type of work	**Estimated hours**
	(not including menu planning)
Shopping:	1.0 hr
Soups/salads x 5:	2.0 hrs
Entrees x 5:	3.5 hrs
Side dishes x 5:	1.5 hrs
Cleanup:	0.5 hr
Packaging and labeling:	1.0 hr
Total hours:	9.5 hrs

Cost of Disposables

Disposables are any containers, plastic wraps, foils, aluminum pans, plastic bags, paper towels, or garbage bags that you use once then throw away. These costs are separate from labor costs and food costs; they are in a category of their own. To accurately charge for these costs, you mark them up by taking what you paid for them and adding on a small cost for gas and labor.

For an example, let's say you buy a roll of aluminum foil and plastic wrap, six rolls of paper towels, and a couple boxes of plastic bags. Your cost is $23.00. If you buy it in the state of California, it will cost you an extra $1.90 in sales tax for a total of $24.90. You now need to add a bit for your gas and time. If you add $2.00 for gas and $3.00 for your time, you will be adding an additional $5.00 to your total, making it $25.60 for you to come out even. You are not in business to come out even; $29.90 is your cost. You add a percentage to this cost, whatever you are comfortable with (I suggest between 15 and 25 percent) to get the amount you pass on to your clients. Twenty-five percent of $29.90 is $7.48. You charge your clients $38.

Because disposables do not last and you are constantly buying them, these can be the items that cost you the most in the end. Typically, semi-disposable containers should be replaced every four to six uses because of stains from acidic food, residue from dishwashing, and distortion from microwave heating. The useful life of Rubbermaid and Tupperware containers is very similar to regular disposables, but they are more expensive because they are often sold as sets. This leaves you with more different-size containers than needed. However, you still charge your clients a range of $50 to $60 or the "marked-up" price of the whole purchase because it is still a part of the cost of disposables.

Pyrex and Corningware are not considered disposables, but they do have a life span and should be replaced every so often, just like the Rubbermaid and Tupperware containers. Pyrex that has a tiny chip or hairline crack (maybe even too small to see) can crack when going from very cold to very hot. Pyrex and Corningware are sold individually at very good prices at discount stores such as Kohl's and Target. Pyrex and Corningware have outlet stores and offer 20 percent on bulk purchases for personal chefs. This is a smart buy only if you have a clientele that will use them.

Keep in mind whether your business purchases are smart ones that can continue to make you money in the long run. Always remember to bill for your time and gas in addition to everything else so you are not working for free.

Reheating Instructions and Nutrition Information

The same markup for disposables applies for writing reheating instructions and nutrition information. In writing reheating instructions, your goal is to make them as easy and efficient as possible for your client to understand and follow.

Mark up your labor costs for the time it takes you to write the reheating instructions on each and every package. If you are typing the heating instructions out for your clients so it is easier for them to read, figure in a percentage of the costs of your printer ink and labels.

For nutrition information, research will have to be done in order to fulfill the needs of your client. It will take you time to figure out substitutions and to calculate the nutrition information. Counting calories and fat and weighing out food for clients with strict diets will take you time. Reading the nutritional labels and facts on food packages in the grocery store will require time as well, so figure in the time it takes you to do this and mark up your labor costs accordingly.

A note about nutrition: You can't trust every nutritional count you read on a food label. Unless you are a certified nutritionist or a registered dietician, don't make nutrition claims to your clients that you can't back up with documentation. Running recipes through a nutritional program does not ensure accuracy.

Accounting Software

If you have trouble keeping your checkbook balanced, you should invest in accounting software to keep you accurate and up-to-date. Below are a few good options. And remember—it's tax deductible!

Quicken 2010 (Deluxe $59.99, Premier $89.99, Home and Business $99.99) by Intuit simplifies tasks like managing your payables and receivables, customizing estimates and invoices, and running business reports. It's the easiest way to see your complete financial picture in one place. It gives you an instant overview of all your unpaid invoices and upcoming bills, and makes it easy to track and categorize expenses with tools and reports like the Schedule C tax form. Monitor expenditures, and keep an ongoing record of tax-deductible business expenses like mileage. Store electronic receipts and tax forms so that you know where they are at tax time. You can even place your company logo on invoices and forms for a more professional look (www.quicken.intuit.com).

Also by Intuit is QuickBooks ($99.95 for QuickBooks Simple Start; $199.95 for QuickBooks Pro). QuickBooks makes repetitive tasks a thing of the past. You enter customer, vendor, and employee information just once, and the program does the rest, prefilling common forms like invoices. It organizes all your important small business information in one place, giving you easy access to a complete picture of your business. Entering transactions is easy because the forms look just like familiar paper forms, making QuickBooks the easiest solution to learn and use (www.quick books.intuit.com).

The Moneydance ($39.99) program allows you to set and track budgets by using easy and insightful reporting and graphing tools. These tools feature automatically balancing your checkbook, tracking charges, managing your budget, and simply organizing your finances (www.moneydance.com).

Computer Software, the Internet, and Training Programs

Personal chef and recipe software is an integral part of running your business and will help you keep track of your clients and what you make for them. The training and software they offer help you to run your business in an organized fashion so you are able to meet each and every client's needs on a personal and individual basis. Whichever software program or training you decide to go with in order to make your personal chef business more efficient, effective, and profitable, keep in mind that you are spending time and money for your clients to be happy with your services. Whether it's organizing their weekly recipes, planning their daily menus, researching nutritional facts for their special diets, or taking classes for recipe procedures or instructional purposes, always factor in the costs of these in order to run a profitable business. Mark up your labor costs a certain percentage for each client so you can cover the costs of running your business productively.

MenuMagic software was specifically designed for personal chefs to help them better run their businesses. Features include menu planning, shopping list generation, printing of customer reports and labels, recipe management, menu costing and billing, customer menu and recipe histories, and recipe dietary exchanges.

Managing menu and recipe costs allows you to see the cost of recipes on a menu and the cost per serving of recipes to help you determine if a menu cost is too high or too low. Menu billing gives in-depth financial breakdowns. Customer trends and histories keeps track of all recipes you've prepared for a customer. With recipe dietary exchanges you can enter exchange information for a recipe in order to cater to clients' dietary needs as well as receive nutritional facts and information on recipes. The selection of reports gives you the option of creating easy-to-read reheating instructions for your customers. For more information visit the website at www.menumagicsoftware.com.

Mastercook allows you to plan menus in advance; create shopping lists for single recipes or entire menus; search for recipes based on specific ingredients, food types, and cooking times; receive expanded step-by-step instructional videos that walk you through recipes; and scale your recipes up or down according to various portion sizes. You can easily manage your collection of recipes in one central location and enter notes and pictures on each one. Keep track of fat, carbs, calories, and cholesterol, and learn about healthy alternatives, nutritional values, and recipe substitutions. Sort your recipes according to your clients' personal needs. Software also includes lessons in essential cooking techniques, ingredient preparation, plate presentation, and details on quick and easy recipe production. There are more than 8,000 different recipes and ideas included. For more information, go to the website, www.valusoft.com, and type "Mastercook" into the search bar.

Now You're Cooking is a computer software program that helps personal chefs organize and maintain recipes, plan nutritious meals, create shopping lists, and manage grocery costs. This program also allows you to import and export recipes at your convenience, refer to the USDA nutrition database for diet restrictions, and print out recipes, meal plans, and lists using an organized personal preference format. For more information, go to www.ffts.com.

The United States Personal Chef Association is a professional organization that provides members with a variety of training and organizational techniques. The first is their Home Study Program specifically designed for the self-learner who wants to work at their own pace. It includes a *Professional Personal Chef Reference Manual* containing more than 400 tested personal chef recipes, and marketing and selling software. The second program is the Quick Start Program, which expands on the Home Study Program. It includes classroom instruction and the MenuMagic personal chef software, as well as the reference manual and more than 500 tested recipes. The third is an undergraduate course that provides the personal chef with more in-depth classroom instruction and kitchen instruction as well as all of the before-mentioned items. You can request an information packet by calling the USPCA at (800) 995-2138, or visit their website at www.uspca.com.

06 Marketing Your Personal Chef Business

What difference does it make if you are the most talented personal chef in town if nobody knows it? Creating your image and telling everyone about it is the definition of *marketing*. Constant self-promotion and continuous marketing are necessary for your success; that's why Coca-Cola still advertises after one hundred years.

Remember that *you* are what makes your business different and special from every other personal chef service out there. You don't just sell your food; you are also selling yourself. You are your most effective marketing tool. What about you makes your service different, better, more unusual than your competition? What knowledge and experience make you special? If you invest the time to learn effective marketing techniques, you'll find that you can turn your ideas and creativity into new business.

Market YOU

Create an image for yourself and tell everyone about it. *You* are what makes your business different from all the rest.

Always search for new markets for your products and services. No matter if business is abundant or slow—create continuous marketing and constant promotion for your business. Marketing doesn't always have to be expensive and difficult. Remember: *You* are the most effective marketing tool you have.

After being in business twenty-five years, I don't even think of marketing as marketing. I just get up every morning and spend some time creating a way to get my company and my name out there. Do I have an engaging culinary story to share on my blog? A funny statistic or picture I can tweet to generate some conversation? Is there a great recipe I should mass-e-mail to my client list? Or a newspaper editor I should call and offer original tested recipes for an upcoming holiday food section? Is there a chamber of commerce breakfast I should be attending and addressing? Or a cooking class I should sell to a local school (Cook Five Dinners in the Time It Takes to Cook Just One)? As a culinary professional, that's something I'm an expert on.

Marketing is about making it easy for potential clients to hear about your services. Sales is about turning potential clients into paying customers.

The Initial Breakthrough

Start thinking about marketing even before you start your business. Ask yourself, "What do I plan on doing that's different, unusual, or essential?" Ask yourself what knowledge, ideas, or contacts you have that will help you sell yourself and your services.

Spend time researching basic marketing techniques. I give you loads of great and inexpensive ideas in this chapter, along with a reading list that will help you get started.

Talk with people close to you about spreading the word about your business. This is basic grassroots marketing, the cheapest and sometimes the most effective kind out there. Don't limit yourself to family and friends; include your church, neighbors, school alumni organizations, children's school, local businesses, and health clubs in your extended network.

The more people you know, the more people will get to know you and the services you provide.

Keeping a Portfolio

Don't forget to take pictures of every menu item you produce. Show these to clients the next time you're on a sales call. Once you've established yourself, expand your portfolio with letters of recommendation, awards, and certifications.

If there was media coverage on your work, include any clippings—it shows great credibility. Put everything neatly into a presentation folder or binder.

Include sample menus in your portfolio and write descriptions of the dishes. Make the descriptions sound mouthwatering and delicious. Your portfolio offers proof that you can deliver on your ideas and creativity.

Defining Your Style, Food, and Credentials

To define your niche, you need to know your local demographics (check your local chamber of commerce website for demographic information). Research the competition, then decide what kinds of clients appeal to you. If you've completed your business plan in chapter 3, you already have much of this information. Studying it will help you to target the clients you want to reach and market your business successfully.

Do some research to discover the different types of personal chefs in your area, then ask yourself these questions:

- How many personal chef services are there?
- Are they full-time, part-time, or seasonal?
- What clients do you think you'd be most suited to?
- Do you imagine yourself preparing elegant fine-dining meals on a weekly basis or ordinary everyday meals?
- What style of service does your competition offer?

To help define your niche even further, you may want to concentrate on who would benefit most from your specific strengths, knowledge, and skills. Someone who is a classically trained chef with a professional culinary background is most likely to have sharper skills and more knowledge than someone who is self-taught with only a basic understanding of cooking. Therefore, the classically trained chef will be able to support a clientele that is more sophisticated in their tastes and, because of the chef's credentials, can charge more for his or her services.

If you are savvy in nutrition, you might want to concentrate on attracting clients with health issues or ones who are on special diets. Having knowledge of nutrition can make your services more valuable to clients with these special needs.

Your Public Image: Your Business Name and Logo

Creating a catchy name and logo is important. This is the first thing potential clients will see, and they will forever associate it with you. It helps if your name and logo reflect your personality, because it is the first tool in marketing yourself and your service. This will be your chance for a great first impression and is primary in building your reputation.

Your Business Name

Choosing a name for your business requires some consideration. Here are a few things to keep in mind:

Finding Your First Clients

Word-of-mouth is one of the best ways to get new clients, but often a slow way. So how did established personal chefs find their first clients? Lisa Brisch and Margot LeRoy, and Pauline Reep all got their first clients from the United States Personal Chef Association's (USPCA) Hire-a-Chef database (www.hireachef.com). Laura Cotton networked with friends and professional connections. Sandy Hall was the first personal chef service in Corpus Christi, Texas, and spent her first year speaking to meetings of any group that would have her.

Marcie McCutchen found her first client through flyers she left at her sister's office. Her second client overheard her talking about it in the restaurant where she worked as a waitress. Jeff Parker worked as an assistant to a personal chef and then put up his own website. Betsy Rogers found her first long-term client through her local Women Business Owners Association.

Brian Ramirez had an article written about him, the first personal chef in town, in the *Detroit News.* Carlin Breinig's first client—a client she still cooks for many years later—came from flyers left at a day-care center. Helena Ess found her first at a new members' reception for the local chamber of commerce. John Bauhs cooked for food cost only for his first client and got numerous referrals.

Linda Page called the two biggest cities in her county and, as she says, "They *gave* me a list of people who owned homes greater than $200,000. They even showed me how to import the data into Mail Merge in Microsoft Word and print the labels." She sent a targeted mailing of her services out to everyone on the list.

Monique Porche-Smith sent out 500 brochures that netted her three clients. Scott Wilson's first client came from a referral by another personal chef—an excellent reason to network with others!

- Make the name simple to pronounce and easy to spell. If it's long or complicated or in another language, people won't chance repeating it out of fear of sounding foolish.
- Look online or in the phone book to see what other personal chef services are named. Who stands out? Who sounds professional and trustworthy? Who sounds flighty, silly, or strange?
- Be careful not to pick a name too similar to that of another personal chef service in town. You'll get each other's mail and bills.
- Consider using your own name: Jennifer Story's Personal Chef Service.
- In most states, fictitious or assumed business names such as *Just Like Mom Used to Make* need to be registered by filing a fictitious-name statement. Many people think that filing a fictitious-business-name statement will protect their use of that name. It will not. You'll actually need to do a business name search to make sure there aren't any other businesses with the same name and then publish a statement in a general circulation newspaper that says you are intending to do business under that fictitious name. This information is then submitted to your local county recorder's office. There are many businesses online that will happily do this for you for a fee.
- Generally, filing a fictitious-business-name statement in most localities will only allow you to open a bank account under that name.

Your Logo

It's not essential that you have a logo, but doing so helps to establish a professional image. If you can't design one yourself, try contacting your local art or design school about hiring a student. Working with a designer to bring your logo to life will also give the designer opportunity to showcase his or her talents. Collect literature with logos printed on them, and look at the ones you like. What do they have in common? Are they colorful? Are they simple? What attracts you to them?

An inexpensive option is to use one of the logos available from printers who do business cards. Some printers have in-house designers who will work with you for reasonable rates.

Look at books on logos, icons, and typefaces. They are full of great ideas and will spark your imagination. Remember that a successful logo not only needs to convey your style, it also needs to grab people's attention.

The Birth (and Rebirth) of a Personal Chef

Resilience: Merriam-Webster's dictionary defines resilience as "the capability of a strained body to recover its size and shape after deformation caused especially by compressive stress. An ability to recover from or adjust easily to misfortune or change."

I knew something about being resilient prior to July 2006, as I had battled (and defeated!) cervical cancer, gone through divorce, and, oh yeah, started the first personal chef service in South Texas back in 2000. But I was still not fully prepared to pack my bags, move over 450 miles away, and start my business (again) from the ground up.

I'd say that I have definitely had some deformations caused by compressive stress in the years since our move! Here is what I expected and the reality of what I actually found:

I assumed that when I left Corpus Christi with a lengthy record of successes in my business, that I knew the formula for success and therefore would have little to no trouble establishing myself in our new location, on the outskirts of Dallas–Fort Worth. I was wrong.

I took for granted that the "big city," which has had a goodly number of personal chefs in existence since the inception of the industry as a whole, would welcome me with open arms. Wrong again!

In Corpus, I had turned away clients who lived more than a thirty-minute drive from me, citing that it was "too far" for the two to three times a month I would see those clients. In my new location I found that unless I was willing to drive a minimum of forty-five minutes in any direction, I could reasonably expect to conclude my culinary career while wearing a paper hat and asking, "Would you like fries with that?" So, I started over in every way possible. I revamped my logo, website, and all of my marketing materials to reflect a more polished and cohesive image. I attended every meeting I could, no matter how few attendees or whether or not they were in my "target market." This meant Lion's Club luncheons, Rotary, Chamber of Commerce memberships—all for the opportunity to give a thirty-second elevator speech about my business and to hand out cards to anyone within arm's reach.

I learned the names and contact information of the editors responsible for highlighting businesses like mine in every newspaper for 50 miles and I sent press releases practically weekly for the first year, hoping to make someone curious enough to follow up. I demoed a friend's high-end pasta sauces in the few boutique grocery stores that carried the products. This was both to earn the small fee provided (after all, self-employed means no work, no pay!) and for the opportunity to chat up scads of potential clients, while wearing my bright green chefs jacket, embroidered with my business name and logo.

I did all of this and much, much more. In other words, I did everything I did when I originally started Dinners on Demand, almost six years before. The one thing that gave me the push to continue trying to grow my business each day while facing a phone that never rang was being able to draw on my experience and see that while things may seem like they will never get better, shockingly, they always do.

I see it like gardening: If you are willing to put in all the work to clear the land, plant the seeds, fight the droughts, the bugs, the rabbits etc., despite it all, your efforts will eventually result in a bountiful harvest. Resilience.

Sandy Hall
Dinners on Demand Personal Chef Service
(940) 255-2020
www.dinnersondemand.biz

How's that for a success story! So impressive and inspirational Sandy.
Thank you!

The most inexpensive way to find a logo is to look at the different icons and characters available in the different style fonts or in free clip art already on your computer or online. You can change their color, size, transparency, and shape with the software you probably already have. If you have a computer with Microsoft Word, you'll have a myriad of typefaces to choose from. The downside of this method is that the likelihood of someone else using the same logo is higher.

Take the time to choose your company name and logo wisely. It's the first step in building your reputation.

Dressing the Part

As with all other aspects of personal cheffing, it is important that you convey professionalism. Wearing proper clothing not only does just this, but is also safer and more sanitary. If you have clothing with your business name and logo printed on it, it's a great source of advertising.

Chef Jackets and Shirts

Many personal chefs wear traditional chef jackets—a uniform that has evolved out of necessity—when they work. The double-breasted jackets can be reverse-buttoned to hide stains. The layers of fabric protect us from spatters and heat. They make us instantly recognizable as culinary professionals.

Many other PCs wear their company T-shirts, polo shirts, or chef scrub shirts. This is perfectly fine as long as you always appear neat and clean. Most wear aprons to protect themselves and their clothing. What you wear depends on how you want your business to be perceived, your cooking style, and what you are comfortable wearing.

Chef Pants

Chef pants are designed to be loose in fit and are made of substantial material to allow for air movement. This makes them cooler, and if you spill hot liquid on yourself, the material can be pulled away from your skin to prevent burns. Try spilling boiling water down your leg when you are wearing jeans and you will see how they *don't* protect you. Patterned chef pants hide stains very well; walking around in obviously stained clothing will do your business no good.

Chef Clothing and Where to Get It

Restaurant supply stores and uniform outfitters usually carry chef clothing, but their selection can be limited. For more to choose from, try one of the online catalogue companies below.

All Heart Chefs

www.allheartchefs.com

Chef, restaurant, and hospitality uniforms and accessories are their specialty. They carry quality apparel and accessories at an excellent value.

Best Buy Uniforms

www.bestbuyuniforms.com

(800) 345-1924

A good place to find inexpensive, basic chef clothing.

Bragard

www.bragardusa.com

(800) 488-2433

Nice selection of chef coats.

Chef Designs

www.chefdesigns.com

Good-quality chef coats and pants. Catalogue available.

Chef Direct

www.chefdirect.com

(800) 789-2433

Great original fabric. Men's and women's pants and jackets in flattering designs.

Chefwear

www.chefwear.com

(800) 568-2433

A full line of culinary apparel. Expertly designed pants, jackets, shirts, shorts, aprons, shoes, and hats all in a great assortment of colors and patterns. Great line of women's chef jackets. Catalogue available.

Culinary Classics

www.culinaryclassics.com

(877) 378-4855

Custom-made chef's apparel with a large selection of solid and patterned fabrics. They have a good selection of women's clothing. Catalogue available.

Trannon Culinary Chef Kits

www.trannonculinary.com

Vaughn Trannon, an executive chef, has created a series of kits that expertly fit all a chef needs when traveling to cook offsite. Gone are the days of schlepping eight Trader Joe's bags! Vaughn's years of experience taught him exactly what he did, and didn't, need to pack to have a successful cook day, and he brings that expertise to all chefs.

Shoes

Chef clogs offer support and slip-resistant soles. They are the traditional choice, but not everyone can wear them. Some people can only wear one particular brand, like Dansko, Alpro, or Klogs USA. Others prefer shoes made for nurses. Some people find athletic or work shoes easier to stand in all day. Whichever works best for you, there are a few things to consider:

1. Are they slip resistant?
2. Are they closed-toed and sturdy enough to protect your feet from spilled hot liquids or a dropped knife?
3. Do they offer sufficient support?
4. Are they easily cleaned? Fabric and suede shoes will absorb spills and odors and get grungy very quickly.

You might get a client who has a "shoe-free" home. In this case, bring disposable hospital booties to wear over your footwear. But, for heaven's sake, don't cook without shoes!

Headwear

It is important that you keep your hair out of your face and out of the food you prepare. Either tie it back or wear a hat. Many chefs prefer color-coordinated baseball caps (put your company name or logo on them). Also popular are skull caps, toques, berets, head wraps, and bandanas.

Whatever you wear, make sure it is clean and looks professional. If you want to create a look that people will recognize, pick a few colors and stick to them. Select a look that fits your business and your personality.

Designing Promotional Pieces

By this time you've established your niche and specialties. You've got your business name and logo. You've got your clientele targeted. It's time to start promoting yourself!

Remember to be consistent with your designs. You want your materials to look like they all came from your company, not from six different companies. Make everything you send out instantly recognizable as yours.

Business Cards

Your business card will be your first promotional piece. Print on both sides of your business card. Don't waste the back; use it to describe what you do, any special skills or knowledge you want to advertise, your credentials, etc.

There are printers you can find online that charge very reasonable rates for color business cards printed on both sides. Companies like Vistaprint (www.vistaprint .com) will even walk you through designing a simple card.

You can print out a card on your home computer. Avery and other specialty paper companies make perforated paper on which you can print your cards yourself. These can look very professional, but may require a bit of printer savvy.

An alternative leave-behind that has proven most successful, even among non-smokers, is a matchbook with your information on it. Find other inexpensive novelties, such as refrigerator magnets, and have your name printed on them (you can even produce these yourself with your computer and printer).

The Yellow Pages

List yourself in the Yellow Pages with an ad that includes your name, your business name (if not your own name), phone number, e-mail, and a brief description of what your services are, along with your motto or slogan, logo, specialties, and length of time in the business.

Brochures

Create a brochure that can fit inside a business envelope; this makes it convenient for you to mail out. Include your name, address, phone number, logo, a description of your services, skills, and knowledge, as well as some quotes from satisfied customers and past clients. Specialty paper manufacturers make brochure paper already printed with color and designs that will go through your computer printer.

Printing an inexpensive brochure or even a postcard is a good investment for personal chefs just starting out. If you are a savvy computer user, there are overnight printing companies like Overnight Prints that will print double-sided 4x6- or 8.5x11.5-inch postcards and ship them to you for very reasonable rates.

You can design your own brochure (see a sample brochure on the next page) on your word-processing software and print out copies on nice paper right on your home printer. This is an excellent option if you are still fine-tuning your service and want to be able to change the content of your brochure at a moment's notice.

What clients are saying about
ON THE RANGE
personal chef service:

Jeff Parker is a highly professional and creative chef. We highly recommend his services!

If you have:
No time or desire to cook
No tolerance for fast food
A desire to eat healthier
Restaurant fatigue*

ON THE RANGE is a unique personal chef service that provides stress free meals prepared to your specifications in your own home.

Your kitchen is left spotless and your fridge is left full of delicious meals!

*A condition caused by too much eating out.

ON THE RANGE
A PERSONAL CHEF SERVICE
Hollywood, CA 90046
www.on-the-range.com

Not just for the rich and famous!

ON THE RANGE
a personal chef service

Delicious,
healthy meals prepared by a **trained chef** in the comfort of **your own home!**

Having your own personal chef is not a luxury reserved for the rich. **ON THE RANGE** can cost you less than eating out at a moderately priced restaurant.

In addition, **ON THE RANGE** will free up 10-12 hours of your time every week to spend in more enjoyable ways.

ON THE RANGE handles all menu planning, grocery shopping, cooking, packaging, and kitchen cleanup.

Your dinners will be cooked by a professional chef right in your own home!

ON THE RANGE specializes in nutritious and fabulous tasting meals. Stop eating unhealthy take-out or salt-laden frozen food!

ON THE RANGE will:

- Customize menus specifically for you and your family

- Do all the grocery shopping

- Buy only the freshest ingredients available

- Make delicious, healthy meals you will look forward to eating

- Take into account any dietary restrictions

- Never add preservatives

- Package all meals conveniently

- Label meals for easy thawing and reheating

- Leave your kitchen sparkling clean

ON THE RANGE
www.on-the-range.com

ON THE RANGE
a personal chef service

Weekly, monthly, or special occasion service available.

For more information contact:
Chef Jeff Parker
chef@on-the-range.com

Menus and price quotes available upon request.

The example on the following page is taken from a brochure Jeff Parker created for his business. It's printed on 8.5x11.5-inch paper, and when it's folded, the back panel is blank except for a return address so that it can be addressed and mailed without an envelope.

Send out recipe cards with trendy dishes or sample recipes of what you would be cooking as a personal chef. Once again, paper manufacturers make postcard paper that will print from your computer.

Getting Good Press

Conduct a publicity stunt, one that makes you look good and is for the good of your community. Research upcoming events at which to contribute your talents. Inform the media about it so they can come and cover the story.

Write a press release of special or interesting things that you think the public would like to know about you or your services. Fax them to industry magazines, past clients, potential clients, and other media sources that can put your services out there to the public.

When sending out anything to the press, always include a promotional kit that gives more information to those who might be writing about you or interviewing you.

Putting Together a Promotional Kit

Promotional kits are handy for two reasons: They can help you land new clients, and you can use them as press kits to gain free publicity for your services from food editors, magazines, and radio shows.

Typically, promotional kits consist of a resume, biography, client list, list of special events you've cooked for, articles written about you, and menus you've created. Use anything about you and your services that will sell you to potential clients.

Organize all of this information in a professional-looking oversize envelope that has your logo on it. Include a small professional photograph (a 5x7 black-and-white photo will do) of yourself so your recipients can feel they know you.

Send your promotional kit to radio stations, local television news programs, newspapers, or magazines for potential appearances, interviews, and story ideas. This can give you great publicity and launch your career.

In putting together your promotional kit, consider what you want the public to know about you. Create a package promoting your talents. If you don't have enough

Writing a Press Release That Will Get Attention

Below is advice from someone who has had years of experience writing press releases: Martha Hopkins of Terrace Publishing (www.terracepublishing.com). She shares what she has learned with us.

Written correctly, effective media releases can catch the attention of the media and generate more coverage for your business than an ad ever would—at a substantially cheaper price. Editors and producers prefer to receive releases that follow a standard format so that they don't have to hunt for the pertinent information. Make their jobs easier by including the following components in your next release:

1. Before you start, make sure you have something newsworthy to say. You don't want to waste someone's time with information they don't care about. Send them news they can use.

2. Audience, audience, audience. Watch the tone and style of your writing to make sure it works for your audience. Journalists want to see factual information. Save your opinions for the editorial page.

3. Indicate the release date. If the release is applicable starting immediately, write "For Immediate Release." If the release should not be used until a later date, write "Hold Until xx/xx/xx" or "For Release on Halloween."

4. Include your contact information flush right on the same line as the release date. It should include your name, phone number, and e-mail. Use bold type for the word "Contact" to make it easy to find on the page. Like this:

   Contact: Martha Hopkins, (254) 644-3505

   martha@terracepartners.com

5. Write a catchy, to-the-point headline. Center and bold the text for a standardized format. Sometimes the title is the only thing an editor will read. If you don't get her attention here, your release may go straight to the trash.

6. List the city, state, and current date at the beginning of the first sentence.

7. In the first paragraph get straight to the point, and answer those five important journalistic questions: who, what, where, why, and when. It needs to have timely, immediate information.

8. In the second paragraph you can go into more detail about your business, your new offer, your event, or whatever you're announcing. To add credibility, quote a client or other reliable source.

9. In the final paragraph provide general information about your business, such as "Terrace Partners is a boutique packaging and publishing firm specializing in cookbooks. They are based in Texas." You can also repeat contact information here as well as important deadlines.

10. To indicate the end of your release, center three number signs below the last paragraph: ###.

11. Format the entire press release in Times New Roman (or another easy-to-read font) in 12-point type. Make sure to double space the text for easy reading.

12. Spell-check and proofread. Nothing will catch the eye of an editor faster than a typo. Take the time to read your work carefully, rewrite anything that's confusing, and correct any errors.

experience to make a promotional kit, then make an attractive package with your ideas and menus that will attract people to your services.

The Constant (and Fun) Task of Promoting Yourself

Don't consider this a chore; it should be a joy, a game, and a challenge. I awaken every day and ask myself, "How can I have fun today, learn something, and make money?"

Become marketing savvy by attending seminars, classes, or training programs on sales techniques and public speaking to hone your competitive edge. Learn how to make offers, sell, and negotiate so you can become a better businessperson.

When selling yourself, learn how to take advantage of the fact that everyone loves to talk about food. Don't be intimidated: Make cold calls to people and businesses that may be able to hire you.

Point out to potential clients how much time they will save by using your services—as much as twelve hours a week in planning, shopping, cooking, and cleaning up.

If you are trained in food safety and hygiene, don't forget to inform people of this. Most back-of-the-house restaurant employees who handle the food have no background in this area. What a scary thought.

Set specific goals for yourself: at least one cold call per day, three introductions to new people every week, and five promotional packages with cover letters to good leads each month.

It often happens that the summer months are slow. People who can afford your services can also afford to travel, and summer is the most popular time for vacations, especially if they have school-age children. Don't let a little downtime scare you. Use it to promote yourself.

Choose marketing tips and techniques that feel the most natural to you so that you make the job of selling yourself fun and easy. Always remember this cardinal rule in sales: Never take no for an answer; just rephrase the question.

Using Your Menus for Marketing

Because food is what you are selling, your menus should be the most important part of marketing your services. Remember, if your clients could cook like you, they wouldn't need to hire you! Make sure they know that you are an expert.

Menus can function as information packets or as great direct-mail pieces. Include sample menus of dishes that you would normally be cooking for a client. You should develop four sample menus, one each for winter, spring, summer, and fall. Or write sample menus for a weeklong meal plan so people will have an idea of what they would be getting for one standard 5x4 service. Have an example of fresh service menus if you plan on offering that service.

Target current and popular lifestyles. If the most recent trend in healthy eating is low-carb diets, then send out sample menus of dishes that are appetizing but low carb and good for you. People always seem amazed when they can eat food that is tasty and still healthy for them.

Send out an e-mail in the late afternoon with a "What's for Dinner?" suggestion. People will have home and dinner on their mind and will be more likely to read it than if they received this e-mail in the morning.

Real-World Marketing Ideas

Many personal chefs find that paid advertising, like newspaper or magazine ads, don't garner them enough of a response to make it worth their while. Word-of-mouth and referrals are still the best way to get business. Having a well-designed and professional-looking website with keywords searchable in Google (see www.google.com/adwords) or www.freekeywords.wordtracker.com is an excellent use of your advertising budget. Websites are discussed in greater detail later in this chapter.

Meanwhile, here are some marketing ideas that have worked well for other personal chefs:

- Teach classes at local kitchen stores.
- Use your car as mobile advertising with signage. Check with your accountant about any additional business deductions. Also, check with your insurance agent to make sure this does not change your insurance rates.
- Ask existing clients to make referrals. You can sometimes encourage this with incentives (like a free entree or a discount on one cook date, or a gift certificate).
- Speak at church groups, events, local career academies, chef groups, and any place that will have you.
- Donate services or a meal to charity auctions.
- Network within neighborhood groups, support groups, school groups, women's groups, business groups, and your children's soccer teams.
- Advertise at gyms, exercise studios, and health food stores.
- Advertise on doctor's office, medical groups, and pharmacy bulletin boards.

- Become friends with a caterer who doesn't want to be a personal chef (provided you don't want to cater). You can send each other the business you don't want.
- Make yourself a walking advertisement: Wear a chef coat and pants with your company name as often as possible.
- Join the local chamber of commerce, Business Networking International, Toastmasters International, or any other group in which you come into contact with busy professionals.
- See if one of the independent grocery stores in your area would let you pass out your business cards at their checkout line. Or offer to create a recipe or two with an ingredient they would like to highlight.
- Advertise in the local Junior League publication.
- Get local newspapers to write a story about your services. Offer to write an article yourself with recipes included.
- Offer to cater an event at cost at which you can advertise your services.

The Internet as a Marketing Tool

Today, the first place someone will go to search for something they need is the Internet. That's why it is to your advantage to have a website educating potential clients about your services.

A website will answer questions potential clients may have, as well as cut back on the number of phone calls you receive that may not turn into new jobs.

Inform potential clients of your experience as well as the products and services you offer. Think of your website as a source of information. Below are some helpful hints in designing your website.

- Don't make people search all over your site for your e-mail address and phone number.
- Helpful holiday tips, new product articles, and changing recipe ideas are an added bonus to your website as they will draw repeat visitors to your page.
- Have a clear and simple website so visitors will not get confused. If their first impression of you is mixed, it may discourage them from doing business with you.
- People love pictures, so include photos of your food, previous events, stock photography, or clip art. Images add interest to your page (make sure they are relevant, not personal).

- If you are not computer savvy, barter with someone to make the Web page and install it for you. Then research a place to host your website, such as your own Internet provider.
- Wherever you decide you want your Web page to live, make sure it is somewhere people can find it. Your site will rank higher in search results if many links lead to your site. Submit your site to multidatabase pages. Find search engines in which you can put in key words that are repeated in the text of your site.

These days, it is not enough just to have a Web page. It is your responsibility to continuously create new content and use social media (namely Facebook and Twitter) to communicate that information. Many people have a blog in addition to (or as part of) their static site as a place for new content, and then broadcast the blog through Facebook and Twitter. Others use their Facebook business page or their Twitter account alone to stay in contact with current and potential clients. Many chefs have blogs only, and have bypassed a static site altogether. Find what works for you, but make sure you work it consistently! There's nothing worse than a blog with your name on it with one entry from six months ago.

Website Content

Your website need not be complicated. It is better to be clear than to rattle on and on and confuse potential clients. Start with something simple:

Jennifer's
Personal Chef Service

Menus customized to your needs and preferences. A week's worth of dinners cooked in just one day.

Organic and seasonal foods are my specialty!

Delicious food prepared by a talented professional chef in your own home.

Call for more information:
310-555-0123
or email me at:
Jennifer@jenschefservice.com

The Power of a Food Blog

You hate marketing. I hear you.

I cringe when I admit this, but I have an entrepreneurial spirit. I wish I didn't. I wish I was content and fulfilled working for someone else who would hand me a paycheck every two weeks, taxes taken out, and hand me my benefits with a smile. Easy! Done!

Unfortunately, every "real job" I ever had left me clock-watching, teeth-grinding, and fantasizing about what I would cook when I finally escaped my cubicle and got back into my blessed kitchen.

Being a personal chef was something I had long thought about but never acted on because I'm a big chicken. I didn't have confidence in my natural cooking instincts and abilities. What did I do instead? I started a food blog. I created my own dream job: cooking, eating, and talking about cooking and eating. All I was missing was income!

I wanted (my imaginary) prospective clients to understand how passionate I am about food, and how better to show that than to create a blog where I post daily. It created a presence and a point of view and showed the world that I am serious and I'm good!

My blog led to culinary school, food writing work, and dipping a toe into the food styling world. And one day, while talking with a friend about my blog, I mentioned personal cheffing. She hired me on the spot and three weeks later her friend referred me to her boss, and I had my second client. Boom.

I loathe marketing. Well, this is not really true; what I loathe is making cold calls, and I thought that was what I had to do in order to market. Not so, my friends! The truth is, there are a million ways to market and once you understand what works for you, marketing can be fun. I swear. With my blog, I market almost every day, in spite of myself.

For me, creating a food blog was the most powerful marketing tool imaginable. It became my calling card, and because I was proud of my blog, I found myself talk-ing it up, which felt much easier than talking myself up. Because of my silly little blog, I have had a (seemingly magical) steady stream of wonderful clients. Who knew?

Blogs can be simple, or not. If I can figure out how to publish a blog, anyone can. Rather than overwhelm myself with trying to make it perfect right away, I told myself just to start simple and clean, and then try to learn one new thing every week. Two years and one thousand posts later, I've learned a lot, and there are worlds more to learn, and that's okay with me. I am honestly excited to continue to learn and grow my blog, my photography, and my culinary prowess for the rest of this life. Nothing could please me more, actually.

Mandy Unruh
Mandy's Meals
www.mandysmeals.com

Mandy is an example of someone who uses all of her talents! Bravo.

Once you've established a website address and put up the first page, you can add more information as you go along.

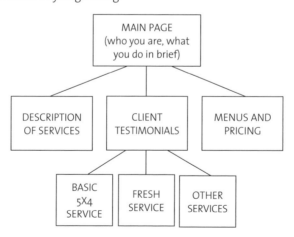

Remember to make it easy for visitors to your site to get the information they need right away.

Other Forms of Advertising

Reach the market you want by doing radio spots, sponsoring Little League teams, and advertising on billboards, in neighborhood newsletters, in city magazines, or on a website.

Continuously keep your name in front of the public eye. Inform yourself about advertising by research, study, and interactions with professionals in the field.

Getting Referrals and Repeat Business

Referrals and repeat business—the name of the game in any business. It saves time, money, and resources when you do business with a previous client. It is also proof positive that you're building a good reputation.

Stay in touch with former clients. You never know when they or someone they know will need your services. Write or publish your own newsletter, and mail it out. Or design an e-mail newsletter or an e-zine—an online magazine that offers handy tips and solutions to your clients. A sample article might be "How to Pack a Tasty and Healthy Lunch for Kids of Every Age."

Plan to send out a new menu postcard quarterly or even ship a new food treat you think a prospective client would enjoy. You can make a flavored salt, package it attractively, attaching a tag telling them how to use it. Put four cookies in a clear plastic candy bag, and tie it with a ribbon with your business card attached. Nobody can resist a cookie, and it's a great way for them to remember your name.

Send out an e-mail blast updating people about you and your services, or simply pick up the phone and say hello.

Tracking Your Success: Are You on the Right Road?

When you get new clients, ask them how they found you. Was it a referral? From whom? Was it a mailing? An ad? Your website? Your card at the local gym? Keep track of the success of your promotional ideas, and stick with those that pay off.

Client Communications

Communication begins the first time you interact with a potential client and doesn't end until you stop breathing. I get calls from clients that I haven't cooked for in years. They saw a new book I'd written or a TV segment I'd done, and sure enough, they just call to say hello.

Meeting Your Clients for the First Time

Lisa Brisch asks her clients why they are looking to hire a personal chef. This helps her ascertain their goals. "On the first meeting we discuss food preferences, favorite meals, how much time they want to spend preparing dinner, and what they currently do for dinner. I also check out their kitchen—making sure their oven is calibrated. If it is off by 25 degrees, I ask them to get it repaired, or they will be disappointed with the reheating of their meals. I give them a folder to keep all the information I give to them." Lisa gives them information on food safety, a sample menu, sample reheating instructions, and her policies on payment, cancellations, rescheduling, menu approval, and kitchen cleanliness.

Laura Cotton makes sure to discuss how much space she'll require in clients' refrigerators and freezers. Most personal chefs have an extensive questionnaire that covers not only clients' likes and dislikes but their lifestyle as well. Sandy Hall says, "This may be the last face-to-face time of any significance that I have with my clients," and so uses this time to get to know them.

Diane Lestina's approach is different. Her initial meeting is "very quick—my clients like to see that I am a professional, but are quite busy and happy to schedule a cooking date" for another time. Marcie McCutchen meets most of her clients online when they place their order. They find everything they need to know about her services from her website.

Jeff Parker, whose background is sales, says, "It's a sales call, first and foremost! Don't ever forget that. If the client doesn't like you, you're out." Brian Ramirez always takes a sample of his cooking with him when meeting new clients. He did this with his first client and before he even got home there was a message on his answering machine from the client "raving about the manicotti and she could not wait for me to come back."

Good communication skills will prevent misunderstandings, make your life much easier, and make it easy for clients to refer you new business. Clients will not refer you if they have been disappointed in your food or your behavior. How many times have you heard, "Well, he [or she] is a brilliant chef [accountant, doctor, hair stylist] but I hated his [or her] attitude."

Effectively conveying exactly what your service consists of is of great importance, as is giving your clients a gracious way to let you know if they are unhappy with something or want to change anything. The truth only hurts for a minute; misunderstandings can fester forever.

Thank-You Notes and Client Comments

Everyone likes being appreciated. Leaving a thank you note to your clients lets them know you value their business and creates an open communication pathway. Purchase nice note cards, and write your thank-you notes by hand.

When leaving behind a client comment card, make sure it is easy to fill out and won't take more than a minute to complete. Fill in any parts beforehand that you can (like the date and client's name).

Customer Satisfaction Survey

PC Laura Slavney says, "I let them know they can call me anytime or e-mail me with any questions." Laura Cotton says, "I request specific feedback—which allows me to fine-tune the service after every cook date—making it personal and unique."

Below are some questions you will want to consider including on a satisfaction survey of your own:

- Are you satisfied with my services?
- If not, what would you like changed?
- Are my menus boring, too spicy, or just right?
- Would you like more or less food variety?
- Are the ingredients I am using tasty and satisfactory?
- Are the portions fitting for you (and your family)?
- How can I make your preparation of the food more convenient for you?
- Are you reaching your health/diet goals with my food?
- If not, what changes do I need to make in order to help you reach your goals?
- Do you feel like you are getting what you paid for?

Thank You!

Dear Ken,

Thank you for using Jennifer's Personal Chef Service. I appreciate your business! Please don't hesitate to let me know if I can do anything to improve my service to you.

Sincerely,
Jennifer Story

Jennifer's
Personal Chef Service

Jennifer's
Personal Chef Service

310-555-1234

Date: _____ *October 15, 2010* _____

To help me personalize your service, please take a moment to fil out the form below. Thank you!

Client name: *Tony and Jackie Meyer*

Portions sizes are	_____ just right	_____ too big	_____ too small
The flavor has been	_____ just right	_____ too much	_____ too little
Were there any dishes that you didn't enjoy?	_____ yes	_____ no

If yes, which ones? _____

Do you have any other comments that would help me make your service better for you?

_____

_____

_____

How to Resolve Client Concerns

Any issues or concerns your clients have should be addressed immediately. As stated above, you should have a client comment card or e-mail feedback system set up so that they can let you know when issues arise. And issues *will* arise. This is the nature of the business. How you handle these issues will affect your entire business.

Personal chef Elizabeth Ozaki notes, "People are a lot more particular concerning food than they are aware of. They may say (and believe) 'Oh, I eat anything,' while quite the reverse is true. We all have our likes and dislikes. They aren't terribly obvious when we are making food for ourselves, but when others do so, our innate pickiness comes to the fore."

Question your clients carefully about their pickiness level.

Hoyt and Lydia Eells do everything they can to accommodate their clients' budgets. "We do not compromise our service or quality. If we can not accommodate the client with their needs, we politely suggest other alternatives."

Handle problems with a view to solving them, not by trying to win an argument or point. Don't (and I can't stress this enough) take complaints personally. Use your head, and figure out the most gracious way to fix the situation. If the relationship needs to end, do all you can to make sure it doesn't end on a bad note.

07

How to Organize Your Day

The first thing to do in organizing your day is to know what has to be done. It's the art of prioritizing. Know which clients you have for that day and what they are going to be eating. When you get their menu approval each week, set up their cook dates, and put their menus on a weekly or monthly master calendar. I hang a huge three-month calendar above my desk. I like looking at the entire fiscal quarter to be able to target days to fill in with work or block out for writing.

Before shopping, take inventory on what dry ingredients you have in your kit and which fresh ones you'll need to shop for. If you have created shopping lists to go with each recipe or menu, it will make your everyday organizing easier. Some of the computer programs discussed in chapter 5 or programs that you can purchase from one of the culinary associations generate shopping lists for you, but if you haven't invested in software yet, do this manually.

When you create a menu or a recipe folder, take a few extra minutes and create a shopping list at the same time. You can keep the shopping list to use again. In creating a binder of selected recipes for your business, keep notes of clients' preferences, cost-effectiveness, and if recipes freeze and reheat well. Protect your recipes and grocery lists by putting them in clear page protectors so you'll have them for a long time.

Allocate your time according to what needs to be shopped for, cooked, packaged, and frozen that day. Cook the more difficult and time-consuming recipes first, then work your way through to the easier ones. Anything that can bake or roast or simmer for awhile should be cooked first; while that's cooking, move on to something else.

If you happen to get everything done for that day, check and see if there are enough ingredients left to rustle up a quick pot of soup to leave as a special treat. I make a seven-minute split-pea soup in a pressure cooker that has soothed many a soul.

If not, go home and work on your setup for the next day. Does your car need gas? Should you go home and bleach your chef jackets? It never hurts to be ahead of your game—you never know what opportunities may come up. Maybe it would be smart to take a taste of that soup to a potential client on the way home from your cook date. Drop off a few business cards, and try to close that deal. I'm always selling. It's second nature to me and has allowed me to stay in business for the last twenty-five years.

Organizing Your Time

Planning your menus carefully will save you time, make you more money, and give your customers greater satisfaction. You want to plan menus that are healthy, satisfying, colorful, comforting, and delicious. And they must freeze well. The easiest way to design menus that fill all of these requirements is to research, cook, practice, freeze, reheat, and eat.

Consider how many recipes you'll need to cook on one cook date. Are you going to cook the standard 5x4 service? In planning your cook date, you want to make sure not every recipe requires the stove top. You only have four burners. Make sure you have some oven recipes that you can be cooking at the same time. You might want a (relatively) quick Crock-Pot recipe and/or a pressure-cooker recipe. I often write at the top of my recipe cards what piece of cooking equipment (oven, stove top, pressure cooker, Crock-Pot, or inside grill) I will need to use. Mix the availability of the equipment on your prep sheet. A prep sheet is just that: a list of jobs for each of your recipes that list the order you need to do them in. See the sample prep list on the next page.

If you've worked in a catering or restaurant kitchen as a chef, you know that you must do many jobs at a time. A chef is a master multitasker. You'll have pasta boiling on the stove, a roast in the oven, a marinara sauce simmering on the back burner, rice cooking, veggies blanching, all while you're mixing up cornbread. The faster you can cook, the more money you will make.

As you get more experience, you'll find tricks that work for you. I always carry a small $200 convection oven in my car when I'm going to cook anywhere. It saves me hours if I need the extra space. It's not too heavy to carry, and I can plug it in anywhere.

Most days I start with the most complicated dishes or the ones that take longest, making easy dishes and sides in between. Stay on top of your dishes, and clean as you go. This is where—if you've opted for a fee-plus-groceries pricing structure—you can really make the most of your time.

When shopping, buy as many prepped or ready-to-use items as possible. A large part of being successful is knowing what great products are on the market. If your clients want every little thing made from scratch, great—you just have to make sure to charge them for your time. But if you're like me and don't mind a good shortcut when it doesn't sacrifice quality, taste-test bottled sauces or spice packets and see if you can't use a few prepared foods to save you time. There are good-quality ones out there.

Sample Prep List

Recipes: Meat Loaf, Mashed Potatoes, and Green Beans

Chicken Stir-Fry

Lasagna and Garlic Bread with Garden Salad

Equipment: Oven, wok or large skillet, broiler

Cooking Time: 1 hour

1. Prep and assemble lasagna.

2. Prep and assemble meat loaf.

3. Put large pot of water on to boil for potatoes.

4. Bake lasagna and meat loaf.

5. Boil potatoes.

6. Cook green beans.

7. Prep and cook stir-fry.

8. Mash potatoes.

9. Cool lasagna and meat loaf.

10. Broil garlic bread.

11. Make salad.

Planning

Time management and organization are the keys to running a profitable and productive personal chef business. Plan which days of the week you will be shopping and cooking, and which days you will be billing and menu-planning.

Designate one day out of your week to menu-planning, developing recipes, doing nutritional research for clients with special diets, and going over dishes with clients. That way, by the time the next week starts, you are well ahead of yourself and can already have your shopping lists ready and know what groceries you need to pick up on what days. This is work I do before I even have new clients or projects. I have created a huge database of tested recipes, most of them original. I like writing recipes and reading cookbooks. I don't even think of it as work. When I need recipes, there they are.

It's always in your best interest to test as many recipes as you can ahead of time. Your cooking will run smoother and more quickly, and the dishes will turn out the way you expect them to. You should collect recipes, plan menus, and write grocery lists all before you start your business in earnest.

Shopping

You already know which recipes you are going to be cooking for a week. All of your menus have been previously priced out, so just combine all the recipes for that week and make one central shopping list. This limits your trips to the grocery store and time spent in the store. Most personal chefs only cook four days a week and use another day to do all of their dry-goods shopping and bookkeeping.

Depending on health codes and regulations in your area, you may not be able to shop for perishables until your cook date, but you can preorder products and have stores hold them for you. On the other hand, you can buy as many disposables and pantry items ahead of time as you have the space to store them.

Buying all of your pantry items at one time and ahead of time, then all of your perishable items as needed throughout the week, is a good time-saver. Preorder items such as meats from your butcher and give him the date you need it ready so you can just go and pick it up. See the sample order form on page 33.

Keep a master list in a small notebook to write down staples you've run out of. Keep this list updated! Make friends with the meat, grocery, and produce managers in the stores you frequent. Ask them when their shipments arrive so you'll know when you will have the freshest and best selection. Ask them for bulk discounts or specials because you can guarantee them daily sales.

Educate yourself about the products you buy. There's lots of information scattered throughout every store. Many products will have a consumer hotline for questions and answers right on the product label. Use them. When I first started cooking and needed quantity recipes, I found free recipes for twelve servings or more available at food boards or councils for particular products. These are food information centers created to educate professional cooks and consumers. Most of the time these boards will send you recipe cards, temperature charts, binders, and sometimes even samples for free. Look in appendix B in the back of this book for a contact list of some favorites.

What Kind of Meat to Buy
Many factors affect the quality of meat that you'll purchase for your clients. When buying meat, external fat should be white, not yellow. Beef and lamb should be red to brownish red, with flakes of intramuscular fat (marbling) throughout. Pork and veal should be fine grained and pale pink.

Season meats with salt and pepper before cooking so that the flavors have a chance to mellow and develop while the meat is cooking. Dry rubs are mixtures of spices and/or herbs that should be rubbed into the meat before cooking as well. Meat can be cooked immediately or left to sit (refrigerated) for up to a day or two. The longer rubs sit on meat, the more flavor the meat will have.

Wet marinades are used primarily for flavor on thin cuts of meat such as sirloin, chuck, top round (London broil), flank steak, and chops. Wet marinades may also be used to tenderize thicker cuts of meat but are not that useful because marinades don't penetrate that far into the meat. No amount of marinating will break down tough cuts of meat, such as brisket or shank. These must be braised or stewed to produce maximum flavor and texture. Do not marinate tender, thin, or small cuts of meat for too long (a few hours is plenty) or it can break down the meat, making it soft and gooey.

There are three major cuts of meat. The first, the top back section, contains the rib, short loin, and sirloin. Steaks and roasts are cut from this section. Filet and tenderloin are the most tender and expensive. New York strip or top loin, porterhouse, T-bone, and rib-eye steaks are just a bit less tender but more flavorful and less expensive. The best way to cook all of these tender cuts is by grilling, broiling, roasting, or sautéing.

Beef

Chuck
Rib
Brisket/Flank
Loin
Round

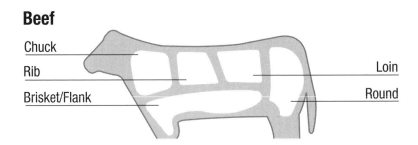

Veal

Shoulder
Rack
Shank/Breast
Loin
Leg

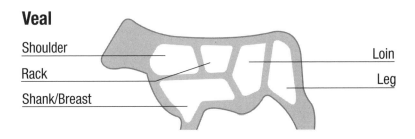

Pork

Shoulder butt
Picnic shoulder
Loin
Ham
Spareribs/Belly

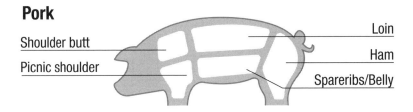

Lamb

Shoulder
Rack
Shank/Breast
Loin
Leg

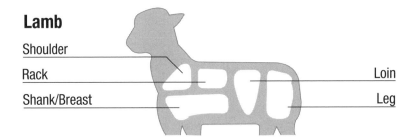

The second major cut is the shoulder and side, giving us the chuck (shoulder), flank, plate, and brisket (foreshank). These tougher cuts are best braised or stewed.

The leg (round), along with part of the chuck and flank, make up the third major cut. These cuts are in the middle of the tough-tender scale. These slightly tougher cuts (like top round) marinate very well. Rump roasts are great slow roasted with dry rubs. Bottom round and round steaks are best braised. Also, all of these cuts are great in a pressure cooker. If you have never used a pressure cooker, go buy one for $39 and get cooking. Nothing to be afraid of except quick, flavorful cooking.

Cooking

Cook things first that you know can hold longer or stay fresh longer, like starches and veggies. Proteins should typically be done last, but if they are labor intensive, do them first and get them out of the way. Have everything measured, cleaned, skinned, deseeded, and chopped that needs to be so the cooking process goes faster. Have all of your ingredients out and ready to go so you can cook efficiently. The French call this your *mise en place,* which means everything prepped and ready to cook; it takes extra time to stop what you're doing to chop something or measure ingredients.

Cook all like ingredients together. Cook all of your vegetables at once, starches at once, and proteins at once. It saves time on production, and it's more sanitary.

Knowing the Basic Cooking Methods

Cooking methods fall into two main categories: moist heat and dry heat. Moist heat methods use water or water-based liquids to conduct heat to the item being cooked. Dry heat methods use hot air, metal, or hot fat to conduct heat.

Most foods cooked in liquid will benefit from seasoning added to the cooking liquid. For example, pasta cooked in salted boiling water will be much more flavorful than pasta cooked in unseasoned water, as will fish poached in a court bouillon (water with aromatic vegetables and sometimes wine). Moist heat methods include:

- *Poaching.* Cooking in a liquid that is very hot but not bubbling (about 160°F–180°F). Poaching is used for delicate foods like fish and eggs out of their shell.
- *Simmering.* Cooking food in water or seasoned liquid that is gently bubbling (185°F–205°F). Most foods cooked in liquid are simmered.

Flavor Essences: The Foundation of Flavor

To maximize flavor is to have aroma, taste, and texture all working together as one. Scientific research shows that there are four basic types of flavor: sweet, sour, salty, and bitter. These are what our taste buds sense when we eat. We have about 10,000 tiny receptors at the nerve endings of our tongues that create these taste buds. When we eat, only 10 percent of any flavor is tasted by these taste buds. The remaining 90 percent is what we "taste" through aroma. This is because our sense of smell is so much more efficient than our taste buds. The more of these four flavors that are present in your foods, the more flavor intensity the foods have.

However, over the years flavor has become more complicated, and studies have introduced four more categories of flavor: pungent, astringent, cooling, and umami. **Pungent** is not sweet, sour, salty, or bitter. It's a spicy and hot flavor that stimulates the taste buds.

Astringent is when the tissues in the mouth contract because of the tannin that is found in foods like unripe fruit, tea, spinach, red wine, and chocolate. **Cooling** is the refreshing, mouth-numbing sensation that develops when we eat menthol, like that found in mint.

Umami is the Japanese term used to describe flavor-enhancing ingredients that heighten the savory flavor of foods, such as mushrooms and monosodium glutamate (what we know as MSG). Umami is known as the flavor of protein because it represents a meaty taste that is not found in any of the other flavors.

Why certain foods taste better than others can depend on a number of things. One is the amount of fat present in food. Fattier foods taste better and have longer-lasting flavor because the fat coats the mouth, prolonging the release of flavors.

A second factor is food temperature. Some foods, like cheeses, are best eaten at room temperature, whereas other foods, like baked goods, are better eaten warm.

Food also tastes better when more of our senses become excited and involved in the eating process. When foods have an array of aromas, flavors, and textures, they taste better than foods that are simple and flavorless. A food that activates only one type of taste bud will taste very flat. Big flavor does not necessarily mean better flavor. Balance is the key when combining two or more flavors because they can cancel each other out and result in a bitter, unpleasant taste. Sometimes less is more.

- *Boiling.* Cooking food in liquid that is bubbling rapidly (212°F). Boiling should only be used for foods that are sturdy enough to withstand the high temperature and constant motion. (*NOTE:* Water boils at a lower temperature above sea level).

- *Blanching.* Very briefly cooking an item in order to partially cook it. Blanching can be done in water or fat. Blanching in liquid is usually done by adding the item to rapidly boiling water, allowing it to cook very briefly, then removing the item and plunging it into very cold or ice water to immediately stop the cooking process. Blanching is done to preserve the color and destroy harmful enzymes in vegetables or to loosen the skins of items like tomatoes and peaches.

- *Steaming.* Cooking foods by surrounding them with steam. The actual temperature of steam is the same as boiling water, 212°F, but steam conducts heat much more efficiently than water, so food cooks much more quickly.

- *Braising.* A slow cooking method in which food is (usually) first browned and then cooked covered in a small amount of liquid. The cooking liquid is almost always used as a sauce after the product is removed. Braising is ideal for items like cuts of meat that are high in connective tissue. The long cooking time will break down tough tissues while the moisture keeps the meat from drying out.

Cooking with dry heat almost always means cooking food without covering it. Covers trap steam and therefore add moisture. Dry heat methods include:

- *Baking/roasting.* Baking and roasting are two different names for essentially the same process: surrounding an item being cooked with dry, hot air.

- *Grilling/broiling.* Fast, high-heat cooking methods. Grilling refers to food cooked by heat produced below the food; broiling refers to foods cooked by heat coming from above the food. Grilling and broiling are ideal for naturally tender foods that would suffer from a long cooking time.
- *Barbecuing.* A roasting or grilling technique that uses the heat from a wood (or coals made from wood) fire.
- *Sautéing.* Cooking food in a pan quickly with a small amount of fat. In order to effectively sauté food, it is important to heat the pan before adding food, to avoid overcrowding the pan, and to avoid shifting the food. These steps will help to create food that is nicely browned, rather than food that has cooked by stewing in its own juices.
- *Pan-frying.* More fat is used in pan-frying than sautéing, and it is usually reserved for larger pieces of food. More moderate heat is used to allow larger items to cook thoroughly. The amount of fat used depends on the item being cooked.
- *Deep-frying.* Deep-fried foods are cooked by submerging them in hot fat. Deep-frying is not a cooking method used often by a personal chef, as deep-fried foods typically do not keep or reheat well.
- *Microwave cooking.* Microwave ovens are an important tool for the personal chef. Precise heating instructions will ensure that your well-prepared food will be enjoyed the way it was meant to be. A few things to keep in mind about microwave ovens:

  - Overcooking is the most common error in microwave cooking. Small items heat very quickly.

  - Use the defrost cycle rather than full power to thaw frozen foods. Lower power allows the item to thaw more evenly.

  - Items that will dry out easily should be loosely covered with plastic wrap or covered in a sauce or gravy.

  - Microwaves heat only the water molecules in food. Items with a high water content, such as vegetables, will heat more quickly than drier foods.

  - Foods at the edges of a dish or plate heat more quickly than those at the center.

Packaging and Labeling

Before you even begin to package and label food for your clients, be knowledgeable about what containers and disposable items are freezer safe, microwave safe (Versatainers), *and* oven safe. Items that are labeled "dual ovenable" are oven and microwave safe. These are items like glass and ceramic casserole dishes, and Pressware (paperboard containers). These types of containers are most convenient because the food can be frozen, reheated, and served all in the same container.

Some Tupperware is microwave safe but not oven safe. Aluminum foil and aluminum pans are not microwave safe, only oven safe. Only certain plastic wraps are microwave safe, so make sure you find out before using them. Freezer bags or Ziploc bags can be used to store food in a freezer and can easily be thawed and emptied into a dish to be heated, but your clients might not want to go this extra step. Refer to chapter 5 for more about disposables.

To make sure your food stays fresh for your clients, it is always best to wrap it in plastic wrap or put it in a thick freezer bag, then foil-wrap it. This causes clients to work harder when reheating their food, though, so they might not want their food packaged this way.

Freezing food in Tupperware, glass, or metal containers is a good idea too. Most of the time the client just has to pull it out of the freezer and pop it in the microwave or oven to heat it. (Putting a frozen glass or ceramic dish straight into the oven can shatter a dish that has a nick or tiny crack. It's best to instruct clients to thaw foods overnight before placing in a hot oven.)

When freezing food, remember that certain foods freeze and reheat differently than others. Make sure that it is safe for the food to be frozen in the first place. Food should be frozen and thawed only once. Don't thaw frozen meat then refreeze it without cooking it thoroughly first.

Certain sauces and gravies made with cheese, milk, or cornstarch will separate when heated after freezing. Foods that have sauces, like pasta dishes, beans, or rice, tend to turn mushy when frozen in a sauce, so freeze the sauce separately. Raw vegetables should not be frozen unless they have been blanched or cooked. Do not thaw frozen raw vegetables then refreeze them, or they will lose any freshness they may have had.

Always cool cooked foods quickly to about 100°F (about body temperature) before packaging and freezing. If you haven't bought an instant-read thermometer

Jennifer's
Personal Chef Service

Vegetable Lasagna 1 serving   Date made: 3/21/2010
Reheating instructions:
Let package thaw in refrigerator overnight.

Microwave on defrost for 6 minutes.

Remove cover and return to microwave.

Cook on high power for 2-3 minutes, or until heated through.

Ingredients:

Whole wheat pasta, fresh tomatoes, zucchini, basil, garlic, mozzarella and ricotta cheese, olive oil, salt, and pepper.

for your kit yet, this is the time. You can buy them in nearly any grocery store for as little as $5.

When labeling your food with reheating instructions, write on a sticky label with black permanent marker, then stick the label on the container before freezing it. If you are typing out the label, follow the same instructions, and make sure the font style you choose is legible and big enough for the client to see. A little tape won't hurt either so the label doesn't fall off in the freezer.

The label should always include the name of the dish, the date it was made, and complete reheating directions. Other things you can include would be nutritional information, ingredients, portion size, date to be eaten, type of meal (such as lunch or dinner), or any other comments you think necessary for your client to know about that dish.

Reheating instructions should say what to do with the dish from the time your client takes it out of the freezer to when they plate it for consumption. Necessary

Dish	Microwave	Oven	Stove
Creamy Soups	2-3 minutes in covered dish for individual portion, 6-8 minutes for four portions	N/A	Low heat until simmering, 5-7 minutes for individual portion, 10-12 minutes for four portions
Stews and Casseroles	3-4 minutes in covered dish for individual portion, 8-10 minutes for four portions	10-12 minutes in covered dish at 350°F for individual portion, 20-25 minutes for four portions	N/A
Stuffed or Layered Pasta	4-6 minutes in covered dish for individual portion, 10-12 minutes for four portions	15 minutes in covered dish at 350°F for individual portion, 20-25 minutes for four portions	N/A
Poultry	1-2 minutes in covered dish, checking every 30 seconds, for individual portion, 5-6 minutes for four portions	5-8 minutes in covered dish at 350°F for individual portion, 12-15 minutes for four portions	N/A
Fish	45 seconds-1 minute in covered dish, checking at 30 seconds, for individual portion, 3-4 minutes, checking every 30 seconds, for four portions	5 minutes in covered dish at 350°F for individual portion, 8-10 minutes for four portions	N/A
Steak	2-3 minutes in covered dish, checking every 45 seconds, for individual portion, 4-5 minutes for four portions	5-8 minutes in covered dish at 350°F for individual portion, 12-15 minutes for four portions	N/A
Sauces	1-2 minutes in covered dish for individual portion, 2-3 minutes for four portions	N/A	Low heat until simmering, 4-5 minutes for individual portion, 6-8 minutes for four portions
Grains	2-3 minutes in covered dish for individual portion, 4-6 minutes for four portions	8-10 minutes in covered dish at 350°F for individual portion, 12-14 minutes for four portions	N/A
Veggies	2-3 minutes in covered dish for individual portion, 4-6 minutes for four portions	8-10 minutes in covered dish at 350°F for individual portion, 12-14 minutes for four portions	N/A

Notes:

Proteins should be cooked until just done so they do not dry out during reheating.

Any dishes with a crust should be heated uncovered in the oven for optimal results.

reheating instructions are whether the dish requires thawing, whether it can be heated in the oven or microwave, the cooking temperature and amount of time until correct doneness, how the client should assemble the dish (whether they can eat it as is or need to add something to it), and serving instructions. Be specific with your heating instructions so that you lower the risk of your client suffering from any unsanitary food handling.

Tips for Successful Freezing

Maintaining the quality of the food you've prepared is an important concern for the personal chef. Freezing is an excellent way to preserve raw and prepared foods, but it should be done properly to ensure that meals make it to the table with minimal loss of color, flavor, and texture.

- Maintain your freezer at 0°F or lower. Cool cooked foods to room temperature, then package and freeze immediately. Placing warm food in a freezer will allow condensation to build inside of packaging as food cools and will compromise the overall temperature of the freezer.
- Liquid or semiliquid foods require air space to allow for expansion. Leave a 1-inch gap between the top of the food and the lid. For nonliquid foods, minimize the amount of air in containers.
- Always clearly label containers with recipe name, date, number of servings, thawing and reheating directions, and "use-by" date.

Laura Cotton: "I think one of the hardest aspects to address is proper thawing techniques. I recommend two days in the refrigerator. Many of the busy professionals have trouble remembering to plan ahead. I suggest they consult their schedule and pull things from the freezer while they're hungry—much easier than after they've dined and are relaxing, or rushing out the door the next morning. Each client receives a 'how to make the most of your personal chef service' tip sheet: information about thawing, reheating, seasoning, etc. What most people find common sense, others have yet to learn!"

- Freeze small, moist pieces of food (such as berries or cut vegetables) on a single layer on a baking sheet before packaging the pieces together in plastic bags.
- Slice cooked meats before freezing. Place pieces of wax paper in between slices.
- Thaw perishable frozen foods in the refrigerator or microwave, never at room temperature.
- Reheat cooked, frozen foods to 165° or higher within two hours of defrosting.
- Choose sturdy packaging that will minimize air contact with food.
- Blanch, cool, and dry raw vegetables before freezing them. This will help preserve color, flavor, and nutrients.
- Freeze foods as quickly as possible. This helps minimize the size of the ice crystals, which will damage the food less as it thaws.
- Unfrosted cakes and cakes frosted with butter-based icings will freeze well; be sure to freeze them uncovered until the icing is solid, then wrap them in plastic wrap. Cakes iced with meringue-based or boiled icings do not freeze well.
- Baked goods can be thawed at room temperature. To revive frozen and thawed breads, bake them briefly in a warm oven.

Cleaning Up After Yourself

"She leaves the kitchen cleaner than it was when she arrived!" is a compliment often received by successful personal chefs. Although it is true that your job is to create delicious food, it is also true that you are working in your clients' homes, their sanctuary from everyday stress. Cleaning the kitchen thoroughly will help reinforce your image as a professional, reassure clients that you are handling their food in a safe manner, and will help you stay organized and on task as you work.

A great tip for getting rid of strong cooking odors from fish or from frying foods is to throw some cinnamon sticks and cloves in simmering water along with any citrus peel you have. Let this simmer while you clean up, and your clients will be greeted with the faint aroma of citrus and spices rather than the faint odor of fish.

Cleaning Tips

- Stay on top of dishes. Load the dishwasher or wash dishes by hand as you work. Letting dishes pile up will make it difficult to keep track of your tools and, worse, will make you look (and feel) disorganized. Unloading clean dishes from the dishwasher will not only make your clients happy, it will prevent you from leaving any of your tools behind.

- Sparkling sinks make a kitchen look extra clean. Baking soda will remove most stains from stainless steel or porcelain sinks, as well as deodorize the garbage disposal and drains. Scrub with a dish sponge, rinse with plenty of water, and dry with a cloth or paper towel to remove water spots.

- Sharpen the disposal blades with ice cubes and running water after cooking.

- Place half of a lemon in the disposal for cleaning after a full day of cooking.

- Wipe out ovens and microwaves with a damp cloth and mild household detergent. Be careful when using harsh cleansers; many appliances have surfaces that can be ruined by the wrong cleanser. Wipe down stove tops and burners, and give enamel surfaces a shine with window cleaner.

- Sweep the floor before you go. If necessary, mop the floor with a solution of warm water and a little window cleaner or white vinegar. This will be safe for most flooring.

- Place a fabric softener sheet in the bottom of your client's garbage each time you change the liner. This cuts down on odors.

- Organize the refrigerator and freezer as much as possible when putting your food away. Arrange your labeled meals as they should be eaten, with the most perishable toward the front. Make sure labels face front. And wipe up any spills.

- Wipe down the fronts and handles of refrigerators, ovens, and dishwashers.

- If necessary, clean the exterior of copper pans with half of a lemon dipped in kosher salt.

- Deodorize if necessary—many people find food smells unpleasant. To get rid of burned food smells, boil a few slices of lemon in a saucepan.

08

Branching Out: Creating Additional Income Streams

There are a few things that you can do in addition to your personal chef service to generate more income. One is to take on some catering and special events jobs. This can be a natural progression, as you already have potential clients at your fingertips: your personal chef clients! Another is to branch out into prepared meal delivery.

If you use your clients' home to cook when you cater for them, then it is all legal and aboveboard. If you are interested in prepared meal delivery, you will need to rent commercial kitchen space.

Creating a Larger Network

Join as many groups as you can. You never know where new business will come from. Membership in a recognized culinary group like the International Association of Culinary Professionals (www.iacp.com) or Women Chefs and Restaurateurs (www.womenchefs.org) can be very useful.

An organization devoted to personal chefs like the United States Personal Chef Association (www.uspca.com) can also help you expand your business.

As explained elsewhere in this book, any group or organization that you become involved with will bring you into contact with potential customers: volunteer work, community organizations, local chamber of commerce, Toastmasters, PTA, school organizations—*anywhere* you can interact with others. And, if you can get a mailing list from the organization, so much the better.

Expanding Your Business

I did my personal chef work Monday through Thursday and then booked nearly every Saturday with a catered dinner party. I could make as much profit from one dinner party as I could for two or more days of personal cheffing. This is a great way to ease into catering: by selling your services to clients you already have.

If you want to expand past what you can handle on your own, you'll need to hire extra help and/or rent commercial kitchen space.

Sharing a Kitchen

When you are first starting out, the most cost-friendly and effective thing for you to do is to find an approved commercial kitchen and share it with another personal chef or caterer. Try to avoid the overhead of a full-time facility. You will only be using the kitchen a certain number of days during the month, and you most likely won't be able to afford it on your own. You may want to run an ad in your local newspaper that specifies what you are looking for exactly.

When looking for a kitchen to share, consider how far or close it is from your home and your clients. Examine the actual layout of the kitchen in terms of size, equipment, and storage space. A well-designed kitchen that best suits your needs will save you time, money, and product. Calibrated ovens, refrigerators and freezers with correct temperatures, thick rubber mats for long hours of standing, accessible storage areas, and ample counter space for prep work are a few of the concerns that can either help or hinder you from running your business efficiently.

In addition, make sure you are not violating any existing lease and zoning laws. Real-estate brokers and attorneys can suggest the right questions to ask and help you work out the best agreement with your landlord.

Your ultimate goal should be to share kitchen space that includes almost everything you need as far as heavy equipment goes. If you are investing your own money to buy kitchen equipment, make sure it is the best so that your food and product can have the most useful life it can possibly have. This can save you a lot of unnecessary time and money.

Renting a Kitchen on a Per-Day Basis

If you find yourself needing kitchen space only a handful of times per month, you may want to check on day rentals from private clubs or churches. Kitchens in places such as these are very often unoccupied and have been commercially retrofitted and approved by the health department. Negotiate a per-day price and use the kitchen only when you need it.

If you are well acquainted with a local restaurant, inquire about using their kitchen during nonworking hours of operation, such as in the early morning when preps and cooks are not there yet.

Outfitting Your Kitchen

Once you've decided on a kitchen, figure out what you will need in terms of pots, pans, and other equipment to do a good job. If you are not already familiar with how commercial-quality kitchen equipment works, visit a restaurant-supply house with the checklist on page 20.

Buy special equipment as you need it for offbeat recipes. A great source for such equipment is industry trade shows.

Hiring Employees

Many people think that hiring family members or friends when their business grows is a good idea. Not necessarily. Do they know exactly what you expect from them? Do they know your rules and guidelines? What should they expect from you? You can't treat family or friends any differently when hiring extra help or you will live to regret it.

The best way to get what you want from anyone you hire is to have what you want in writing. You will probably be hiring someone to help you on a job-by-job basis, especially if you branch out into catering.

Accepting a Position as a Full-Time Private Chef

What do you do if someone offers you a full-time position to cook for them five days a week? What if they wave too much money in your face to refuse? It happened to me, and it can happen to you too. I'll tell you right now: It's easier having lots of clients than just one client. There is a danger of becoming another one of their servants rather than a respected professional. It completely depends on the client and how they view you and your position in their household.

One personal chef I know quit an excellent-paying private chef job when the client failed to understand why he wouldn't pick up her dry cleaning or take her dog to the groomer. Another good friend of mine is a private chef for a very wealthy family. He is paid through the family foundation and is considered an employee of the foundation, which means he receives vacation and sick pay, medical benefits, and a pension. The household staff is so large that he is considered a professional just like the security people and the pilot.

Another woman I know has been the private chef for a family for many years. They have houses in different parts of the world and take her with them when they spend time there. She has become a valued part of their family.

A private chef who works in Los Angeles and has had a string of celebrity clients complained to me that the meals requested of him from one client were generally scrambled eggs and hamburgers. His clients were rarely home, but their many children were, and it was his job to cook what they wanted. Another LA private chef told me she was "really sick and tired of cooking the same thing over and over again for people with undeveloped palates," but that the money was too good to turn down.

It all has to do with the dynamic between you and your employer. I would strongly suggest that you do this on a trial basis, say two weeks, before you agree to anything longer. It could be rewarding, fun, and a great adventure. Or it could be cold, lonely servitude. But good or bad, it will definitely be interesting.

Catering and Special Events

Understand that as a caterer you are operating under different regulations than as a private chef. Just as with a PC service, caterers are not allowed to cook from their home kitchens and deliver food to the client. Until you find a commercial kitchen you can rent, the best thing you can do is cook from the client's home. This is the best option if your catering jobs are infrequent. That being said, catering is an excellent way to make extra money. Your biggest sources of clients are *already* your personal chef clients.

If you specialize in smaller events (fewer than thirty people), you can target the clients that bigger catering companies won't bother with. As a caterer you should be able to handle a buffet-style party for fifty with just one extra pair of hands (see my *How to Start a Home-Based Catering Business* book for more information). Because your company is only you, you can take on last-minute catering jobs. Two days' notice is plenty of time to get everything together.

At the beginning of my career I could make elegant sit-down dinners for six people that would make me a nice profit. I'd hire a waiter for more than six people. This allowed me to charge around $75 per person (give or take $10) and made me an excellent profit of at least 50 percent.

For your first catering jobs you may want to hire that extra pair of hands—someone to help you set up, help keep the food refreshed, help pick up used plates and things, and help clean up in the kitchen. Until you know how much work you can do yourself, it's really nice to have the extra assistance.

The Necessities of Networking

By nature, I would rather sit in the back of the room and observe. However, running a personal chef business can be lonely and daunting. I have found that it is necessary to network and get the word out there. Follow your own personality (there are a million ways to market your business), but challenge yourself to think outside the box.

In the spring of 2008, I found myself approaching the front door of a mansion in Tacoma, Washington. Inside this mansion were a group of business professionals, attending a half-day publicity workshop. I was sweating under my black dress, obsessively rehearsing in my head what I would say. This was my first experience with networking in the "real world." Up to this point, I had been getting together for meetings with other local personal chefs. This is good to do, of course, but these chefs were not potential clients! Immersing myself in this publicity workshop was the first step in my networking journey.

We were asked to wow our audience with a sixty-second elevator speech. Holding a microphone (gulp), I don't even remember what I said that day, but the feedback afterwards was amazing. You would think that a personal chef was some sort of celebrity! Everybody wanted to talk to me, and I learned that people love to talk about food and to learn new things about food.

After this first experience, I was ready to explore. I sought out local networking groups, ranging from professional associations (National Association of Catering Executives or NACE, Women Chefs & Restauranteurs or WCR, and The American Culinary Federation or ACF) to small business "coffee clubs." I learned that each group had its own protocol and etiquette. At NACE meetings in my area, for example, we mingle socially with other catering professionals. During the program, we stand and say who we are and describe our service. The coffee club I attend is open to all types of small business owners. Most networking groups will also ask that you bring enough promotional materials, such as business cards or brochures, to pass around to each attendee.

Through both types of networking groups, I have received tremendous benefits. I have formed partnerships with a local wine merchant, teamed up with massage therapists to provide in-home dinner and massage events or parties, and best of all, through a chain of events and relationships that have been nurtured through networking, I will be moving into a commercial kitchen facility that will allow me to service more clients in my personal chef business and take on more catering events. These opportunities would not exist had I not opened my mouth and said hello!

- **Look for local networking groups.** You should be able to attend at least one meeting without becoming a member.

- When you find a group (or groups) you are comfortable with, become a member! Oftentimes, there are added benefits, such as being included on the group website.

- **Find a publicity specialist.** At the very least, sign up for e-mail newsletters and start reading the specialist's blogs, if they have one (and they will). Choose to spend a few dollars and take the workshops that are offered. This shows that you are treating your business seriously. As personal chefs, the more exposure we get, the better it is for our industry.

- **Love the Internet.** First, create your website! In addition, be active on association message boards, build a Facebook fan page, open a Twitter account, etc. Support your fellow personal chefs and support the other business owners you meet as you are involved in networking groups.

- **Use the press.** I have sent out press releases related to charity work I have done as a personal chef. As a result, numerous articles were written about me, which led to other job opportunities that were not only lucrative, but also personally fulfilling.

These days, I am asked to guest-speak regularly at a local culinary arts school regarding the importance of networking and marketing. I actually was a student in this program and they brought me back to speak because the instructor told me that I was the "best networker he knew." Me? The girl who would slink down in the back row to avoid talking to anyone? I have realized through all of my experiences that, for me, the Golden Rule is to develop relationships and maintain them. You will meet many people as you start branching out to network. Be professional, friendly, and use common courtesy as you come in contact with new people. Maintain these relationships when it is practical to do so. You never know who you may be able to help in the future (or who can help you!).

I still get nervous when facing groups. However, my confidence has grown exponentially because I believe what I have to say is relevant and my desire is to help people. I let my personality shine when I am in these groups. The friendships I have formed are very dear to me, and this, my dears, is all thanks to networking.

Sara Myron
Gig Harbor, WA
(253) 225-4452
www.personalchefscooperative.com

Sara—you are smart and lovely—who wouldn't want to listen to you?

09

Menus and Recipes

All of the following recipes serve four.

Comfort Food Menu

Comfort food reminds us of being taken care of, of being children. Comfort food means different things to different people. Here is a menu that transcends territorial boundaries. Use turkey instead of beef for a healthier meat loaf; add your client's favorite veggies to the soup, or use half-and-half or cream instead of milk for richer mashed potatoes.

Fresh Vegetable Soup

2	tablespoons butter
1	medium onion, diced
2	cups chicken stock
4	cups water
1	bouquet garni (bay leaf, oregano sprigs, parsley sprigs, lemon zest strips)
1	pound plum tomatoes, skins and seeds removed
1	medium carrot, peeled and thinly sliced
3	medium red potatoes, cut into 1-inch cubes
2	stalks celery, thinly sliced
1/2	teaspoon salt, or more to taste
	freshly ground black pepper to taste
1	ear yellow corn
1/4	pound small green beans, trimmed and sliced

In a large saucepan over medium-low heat, melt the butter. Add the onion and sauté, stirring, until translucent, 3–4 minutes. Add the chicken stock and water. To assemble a bouquet garni, gather together a bay leaf, oregano

Making Your Own Stock

Stock and broth are made by cooking meat, fish, or vegetables in water and straining out the added solids. The difference in today's cooking world between stock and broth is that broth is typically thought of as a canned or store-bought product and stocks are considered to be homemade. Before the convenience of so many canned products, stock was a component made in professional kitchens to flavor-boost their sauces or soups, and broth was actually a finished product that could stand alone. It is wonderful to be able to make your own stock when time allows. If not, buy the best canned or boxed stock you can. Be sure to check the sodium contents and buy the lesser.

Brown stock is made with bones that have been roasted, which provides a lot of flavor and body to the liquid.

Basic Chicken Stock. Put a large whole chicken in a large tall pot. Add just enough cold water to cover by 1 inch. Add a pinch of salt to start. Keep over a low heat, being careful not to boil (this allows all impurities to float to the top). Skim away impurities with a large spoon, and add 1 coarsely chopped onion, 1 large coarsely chopped carrot, and 2 coarsely chopped celery stalks. Also add a bouquet garni (see sidebar) and simmer for 3–4 hours. Strain stock through a fine mesh strainer, and let cool. A fat layer will form on the top, which can easily be removed after stock has cooled and fat solidifies.

Basic Beef Stock. Follow the same directions as for the chicken stock above using an inexpensive, tougher cut of beef instead of chicken. The tougher the beef, the more flavor and body your stock will have. Adding well-roasted beef bones to your stock will make it extremely flavorful. Beef stocks should be simmered for 4–5 hours.

Basic Vegetable Stock. Use the same directions as for chicken stock, but use more vegetables. Adding bay leaves, parsley, and thyme will flavor your stock well.

You can also use leeks, mushrooms, and parsnips for flavor. For a more intense vegetable stock, roast the vegetables before use.

Quick Chicken Stock. A quick way to make a chicken stock is to use leftover roasted chicken or chicken trimmings, bones, and skin. Add onions, celery, carrots, and a bouquet garni. Cover with water, and cook 1 hour. Strain and cool. Another quick way to make chicken stock is to add vegetables, herbs, and seasonings to store-bought broth and simmer for 1 hour before straining. Only use low-sodium premium broths for this purpose (other kinds contain too much salt).

Turning Stock into a Glace de Viande. Stocks can be turned into a *glace de viande* (French for "meat glaze") by cooking stocks down to reduce the liquid to a syrup. This can be added to sauces, soups, or stews to give them a richer and deeper flavor and color. You can freeze glace de viande in ice cube trays, then store in freezer bags. It will keep for up to 1 year.

sprigs, parsley sprigs, and lemon zest strips, and tie securely with kitchen string. Add to the pan along with the tomatoes, carrot, potatoes, celery, and the salt and pepper to taste. Bring just to a simmer over medium-high heat, then reduce the heat to low, cover, and simmer for 20 minutes.

Firmly hold the ear of corn, stem end down, on a cutting surface, and using a sharp knife, carefully cut off the kernels. Add the kernels to the soup along with the green beans and continue to simmer, covered, for another 15 minutes.

Remove and discard the bouquet garni. Taste and adjust the seasonings. Serve very hot.

Meat Loaf

1	pound lean ground beef
1/2	pound ground veal
1/2	pound ground pork loin
2	tablespoons canola oil
1	medium onion, chopped
1	stalk celery, chopped
1/2	red bell pepper, chopped

2	tablespoons fresh oregano, chopped
$3/4$	cup panko bread crumbs
$1/3$	cup milk
1	egg, lightly beaten
$1/4$	cup red wine or beef stock
$1\frac{1}{2}$	teaspoons salt
	freshly ground black pepper to taste

Preheat the oven to 375°F. Grease a $1\frac{1}{2}$- or 2-quart loaf pan or baking dish and set aside.

In a large bowl, combine ground beef, veal, and pork. Mix together and set aside.

Place oil in a sauté pan over medium heat. Add onion, and sauté for 1 minute. Add celery, bell pepper, and oregano. Reduce heat to low, and simmer for 4–5 minutes.

Place bread crumbs in a small bowl. Sprinkle milk over bread crumbs. Let stand a few minutes.

Add onion mixture, bread crumbs, and egg to meat mixture. Stir to combine. Season with salt and pepper. Form into a loose loaf, and place in prepared loaf pan. Pour wine or stock over loaf. Bake uncovered until cooked through, about $1\frac{1}{2}$ hours. To test for doneness, insert an instant-read thermometer into center of the loaf; it should read 165°F. Remove from the oven, and cover loosely with foil. Let rest for 5–10 minutes before slicing.

Mushroom Gravy

4	cloves garlic, minced (optional)
2	tablespoons butter
1	small onion, minced
1	pound mushrooms, sliced
1	tablespoon soy sauce
$1/2$	cup red wine or beef stock
1	tablespoon balsamic vinegar
1	tablespoon cornstarch dissolved in $1\frac{1}{2}$ cups cold water
$1/2$	teaspoon sugar
2	tablespoons fresh parsley, chopped

Sauté garlic in half the butter over low heat for 2 minutes. Remove garlic from pan, and set aside. Sauté onion over medium heat until golden, about 7 minutes. Remove onion from pan, and set aside. Increase heat to high, and add mushrooms to pan with remaining butter. Sauté mushrooms until golden.

Return garlic and onions to pan. Add soy sauce, wine or beef stock, and vinegar. Bring to a boil, and cook until liquid has evaporated. Whisk cornstarch mixture, and add to pan, along with sugar. Bring to a boil, stirring constantly. Reduce heat, and simmer 2 minutes. Stir in parsley. Season with salt and pepper.

Mashed Potatoes

3	pounds russet potatoes
6–8	cloves roasted garlic (optional)
6	tablespoons butter, cut into small pieces
1–1½	cups whole milk, warm
	salt and freshly ground black pepper to taste

Bring a large pot of water to a boil. Meanwhile, peel the potatoes and quarter them. Add the potatoes and garlic (if using) to the pot, and return to a boil. Gently boil the potatoes until tender, 15–20 minutes. Drain in a colander.

Force the warm potatoes and the garlic (if using) through a ricer or food mill into a large bowl. Add the butter and stir with a wooden spoon, letting the butter melt completely. Add 1 cup of the hot milk, and gently stir with a wooden spoon to incorporate, adding more milk to thin to the desired consistency. Add salt and freshly ground black pepper to taste.

Bouquet Garni for Fabulous Flavor

The term *bouquet garni* refers to either a bundle of fresh herbs tied together with kitchen twine or dried herbs and spices tied up in a bit of cheesecloth and immersed in cooking liquid to add flavor and aroma. It can be easily removed when you are finished cooking. There is no rule about what to use in a bouquet garni, but the traditional version is a bay leaf tied up with a few sprigs of fresh parsley and thyme. Sometimes a small carrot, stalk of celery, lemon or orange peel, or leek is added. If you use cheesecloth, you can add whole spices like peppercorns, cloves, allspice, or juniper berries, as well as dried herbs. Try adding a few dried mushrooms for fabulous flavor. The only limit to what you can use is your imagination!

Kid-Friendly Menu I

Bocconcini (meaning mouthful in Italian), bite-size balls of mozzarella about the size of cherry tomatoes, make this a fun salad for kids. They can eat the salad and the chicken fingers all with their fingers. If your clients' kids are not broccoli fans, use another green vegetable, such as green beans or raw spinach.

Cherry Tomato, Bocconcini, and Broccoli Salad

1	pint cherry tomatoes
1	pound bocconcini
2	cups broccoli florets, blanched
2	tablespoons extra virgin olive oil
	salt and freshly ground pepper to taste

Place all ingredients in a bowl and toss.

Oven-Fried Chicken Fingers

- 2 large eggs, beaten
- ½ cup low-fat mayonnaise
- 2 tablespoons Dijon mustard
- 2 cups panko bread crumbs
- ½ teaspoon ground thyme or 1 teaspoon fresh thyme
- 1 teaspoon salt
- 1 teaspoon freshly ground black pepper
- ½ teaspoon ground oregano or 1 teaspoon fresh oregano, chopped
- ½ teaspoon garlic powder
- 4 chicken breasts, boneless and skinless, cut against the grain into 1/2-inch strips

Preheat the oven to 400°F. Place a wire rack on a baking sheet.

In a shallow bowl, whisk together eggs, mayonnaise, and mustard. In another shallow bowl, mix bread crumbs, thyme, salt, pepper, oregano, and garlic powder.

Dip chicken in mayonnaise mixture, then roll in bread-crumb mixture. Place on wire rack. Don't crowd chicken pieces.

Bake for 20 minutes, or until chicken is cooked through.

Fresh Chunky Applesauce

- 1½ pounds Granny Smith apples, peeled and chopped
- 1½ pounds Fuji or Gala apples, peeled and chopped
- 1 cup water
- 1 cup apple cider or juice
- 1 tablespoon fresh lemon juice
- ¼ cup golden raisins (optional)
-   zest from 1 lemon
- ⅓ cup sugar
- ½ teaspoon ground cinnamon
- ¼ teaspoon ground cardamom (optional)

Combine apples, water, apple cider or juice, and lemon juice in a large saucepan. Bring to boil over high heat. Reduce heat to medium, cover, and simmer until apples are very soft, about 20 minutes.

Uncover, add raisins and zest, and simmer until mixture is thick, stirring frequently, about 10 minutes. Remove from heat.

Mash apples slightly. Stir in sugar and spices. Taste and add more lemon juice if desired.

Kid-Friendly Menu II

What kid doesn't like the childhood classic dish of mac and cheese? The healthier alternative to tortillas using lettuce leaves gives this menu a fun twist to food that kids and parents alike love to eat. Give the lettuce wraps an Asian flair by using ground turkey, sesame oil, soy sauce, red bell peppers, and cilantro with butter lettuce.

Crunchy Cole Slaw

1/2	pound green cabbage, shredded
1	cup fennel bulb, thinly sliced
1	cup carrots, shredded
1/4	cup low-fat mayonnaise
1	tablespoon fresh lemon juice
	salt and freshly ground black pepper

Mix all ingredients together in a bowl and chill.

Turkey Taco Wraps

1	tablespoon olive oil
1/3	cup red onion, minced
1	pound ground turkey
1	packet taco seasoning
1/2	teaspoon salt
1	medium tomato, chopped
1/3	cup green onions, sliced
1/4	cup fresh cilantro, chopped
1	cup shredded cheddar cheese
1	head butter or limestone lettuce
	sour cream and salsa for garnish

Place a large sauté pan over medium-high heat. Add oil and onions, and cook for 3–4 minutes or until onions are soft. Add turkey, and sauté until brown, about 5 minutes. Add seasoning blend and salt. Cook for an additional minute. Remove from heat, and stir in tomato, green onions, and cilantro.

Spoon some turkey mixture and cheese onto lettuce leaves. Roll up, leaving top open but folding bottom up so they can be picked up and eaten by hand.

Serve with sour cream and salsa.

Mac and Cheese

1½	cups milk
2	whole cloves
½	small onion
2	tablespoons unsalted butter
2	tablespoons all-purpose flour
1½	cups shredded cheddar cheese
	salt and freshly ground black pepper to taste
	pinch ground nutmeg
1	pound elbow macaroni, cooked
1	cup panko bread crumbs

Preheat the oven to 325°F. Grease a 2-quart baking dish.

In a saucepan over medium heat, combine milk and cloves and onion. Bring to a simmer. Remove from heat, and set aside for 10–15 minutes.

Melt butter in a saucepan over low heat. Whisk in flour and cook, stirring constantly, for 30–40 seconds. Remove from heat.

Remove cloves and onion from milk and discard them.

Gradually pour milk into flour mixture, stirring constantly until smooth. Return to heat and slowly bring to a boil, stirring until sauce thickens and is smooth, about 3–4 minutes. Add ½ cup of the cheese, and stir until blended. Stir in nutmeg.

Add salt and pepper to taste.

Spoon the sauce over macaroni and scatter with remaining cheese and bread crumbs. Bake uncovered until lightly browned and bubbling, 25–30 minutes.

Time-Saving Gadget

This is a great tool to have in your box of magic tricks. It's called a julienne peeler, and it looks like a hefty vegetable peeler with one of the blades serrated. Use it to make perfect julienne of any length. It works best on firm vegetables like potatoes, cucumbers, carrots, jicama, and parsnips.

Classic Kitchen Menu

The timeless elegance and simplicity of a roasted chicken, mashed potatoes, and a soup or salad is a traditional meal ideal for any time of year. As a variation, substitute yellow squash or eggplant for the zucchini ribbons. Use other fresh herbs for the roasted chicken, like thyme or herbs de Provence.

Roasted Rosemary Chicken

1	(3-pound) whole chicken
1	big bunch whole fresh rosemary, 1 tablespoon chopped
	salt and freshly ground pepper to taste

Preheat oven to 400°F. Remove the insides from the chicken, and wash interior and exterior thoroughly. Pat dry.

Lightly oil a roasting pan. Sprinkle the whole outside and inside of the chicken with salt and pepper. Stuff chicken with whole fresh rosemary sprigs, and sprinkle the chopped rosemary evenly on the outside.

Place chicken breast-side up in the pan, cover loosely, and bake about 40 minutes, until chicken renders clear juices and reaches an internal temperature of 170–175°F. Uncover, and cook for the remaining 20 minutes until skin is golden brown and crunchy.

Zucchini Ribbons

2	cloves fresh garlic, minced
2–3	tablespoons extra virgin olive oil
3	zucchinis, thinly sliced lengthwise ⅛ inch thick
	salt and freshly ground pepper to taste

In a sauté pan over medium heat, cook the garlic in the olive oil about 2 minutes, until tender and fragrant.

Add the zucchini ribbons with salt and pepper to taste. Cook about 3–5 minutes, until the zucchini is lightly brown and semitender.

Remove from heat and serve immediately.

Garlic Mashed Potatoes

1	head garlic
1/4	cup extra virgin olive oil
2	pounds Yukon gold potatoes, washed, peeled, and cut into large cubes
4	tablespoons butter
1/2	cup milk
	salt and freshly ground pepper to taste

Preheat oven to 400°F. Cut off root top of whole head of garlic about 1/2 inch so it is open faced. Place garlic in a small baking dish, and drizzle with extra virgin olive oil. Lightly sprinkle with salt and pepper. Cover and bake for about 45 minutes to 1 hour, until whole head is tender and fragrant. Remove from oven and olive oil, and let cool. Squeeze cloves out of the skin, and set aside.

Cook potatoes in boiling water until completely tender but not mushy. Drain under cold water.

In a saucepan, heat together the butter and milk.

Hand mash or lightly puree the potatoes and garlic together. Gradually work in the butter and milk mixture until desired thickness and consistency are reached. Salt and pepper to taste.

Cream of Broccoli Soup (minus the cream)

2	tablespoons extra virgin olive oil
2	cloves garlic, minced
1/2	pound cauliflower, florets and stems trimmed and coarsely chopped
1	pound broccoli, florets and stems trimmed and coarsely chopped
8	cups chicken stock
1/2	teaspoon salt, or to taste
2	teaspoons Dijon mustard
1	tablespoon fresh tarragon or 1 teaspoon dried
	freshly ground black pepper

Heat oil in a large pot over medium heat. Add garlic and sauté for 1 minute. Add the cauliflower, broccoli, stock, and salt. Bring to a boil. Reduce heat, and simmer until vegetables are tender, about 20 minutes. Stir in mustard and tarragon. Remove from heat, and let cool slightly.

Working in batches, transfer into a blender or food processor, and process until smooth. Taste and adjust seasoning. Thin with stock or water if too thick.

Steak and Arugula Salad

- 1 tablespoon balsamic vinegar
- 1 teaspoon Dijon mustard
  salt and freshly ground black pepper
- 3 tablespoons plus 1 tablespoon extra virgin olive oil
- 4 ounces arugula
- 1 pint cherry tomatoes cut in half
- 1 pound beef tip steak
  Parmesan shavings

Whisk together vinegar, mustard, salt, and pepper in a large bowl. Whisk in 3 tablespoons olive oil. Add arugula and tomatoes, and toss to coat.

Season steak liberally with salt and pepper. Heat remaining oil in a large sauté pan over medium-high heat. Cook until browned, about 5 minutes on each side, depending on thickness. Place steak on a cutting board, and allow to rest for 3 minutes. Slice steak thinly, and arrange over arugula. Top with Parmesan shavings before serving.

Punch Up the Flavor with Roasted Garlic

When garlic is roasted, it has a sweet nutty flavor and a creamy consistency. Adding roasted garlic to nearly any recipe will add depth of flavor and mellowness without the sharpness of raw garlic. And it's easy and inexpensive. Start with a whole head of garlic. Using a serrated knife, slice off the top third of the head. Drizzle with a little olive oil, and sprinkle with salt and pepper. Replace the top of the head, and place and wrap in foil. Place in a 375°F oven, and bake until garlic is soft, about 45 minutes. When cool enough to handle, unwrap and squeeze out the soft pulp. Use to flavor soups, stews, salad dressings, or stuffing. Rub on meat, chicken, or fish before cooking, or combine with stock, wine, or butter and use as a sauce. Toss cooked vegetables with a little melted butter, roasted garlic, toasted nuts, and a sprinkling of sea salt.

Low-Carb Menu

For those of you who have carb-conscious clients, this high-protein menu is a sure-fire way to satisfy their appetites and taste buds. To give them variety, substitute their favorite meats and vegetables for the piccata and Parmesan-crusted veggie.

Spinach Salad with Bacon, Tomato, and Avocado

1	(10-ounce) bag prewashed spinach
4	plum tomatoes, quartered
1	ripe avocado, sliced
1/2	pound bacon, cooked and crumbled
1/2	cup salad dressing (ranch or blue cheese work great)

Combine all ingredients and serve.

Veal Piccata

1 1/2	pounds veal cutlets, about 1/4 inch thick
	salt and freshly ground black pepper
1/4	cup all-purpose flour
1	tablespoon plus 2 tablespoons extra virgin olive oil
2	cloves garlic, minced
1/2	cup chicken stock
1/3	cup fresh lemon juice
1 1/2	tablespoons capers, rinsed and drained
2	tablespoons fresh parsley, chopped

Season veal with salt and pepper. Dredge veal in flour to coat both sides. Shake off excess.

Heat 1 tablespoon olive oil in a large sauté pan over medium-high heat. Cook veal in batches until lightly browned, about 1 1/2 minutes per side.

Heat remaining oil in the same skillet. Add garlic and cook until fragrant, about 30 seconds. Add stock and lemon juice, and stir, scraping up any browned bits, and bring to a boil. Cook until liquid is slightly reduced, about 3 minutes. Stir in capers and parsley. Serve over veal.

Parmesan Crusted Cauliflower

- 1 head cauliflower
- 2 tablespoons extra virgin olive oil
- 1 large egg
- 1 tablespoon whipping cream
- 2 cups freshly grated Parmesan cheese

Preheat oven to 400°F.

Slice cauliflower into very thin wedges, keeping the pieces no thicker than ½ inch. Save any bits of cauliflower that break off.

Spread oil on a nonstick baking sheet or on a parchment-lined baking sheet. Set aside.

Beat egg with cream in a shallow bowl. Spread cheese on a plate. Dip cauliflower wedges into egg mixture, then press into cheese. Lay cauliflower on prepared baking sheet.

Mix broken cauliflower with remaining eggs and cheese. Drop by small spoonfuls onto baking sheet, flattening slightly.

Bake for 15–20 minutes or until browned on the bottom and easy to turn without cheese sticking to baking sheet. Turn over, and bake for 10 minutes longer.

Low-Fat Menu

For a high-protein addition to your clients' low-fat diet, add grilled chicken or turkey to the Caesar salad. Try collard greens, mustard greens, or escarole in place of the kale. Black-eyed peas are a perfect complement to all three of these leafy greens.

Emulsions Explained

An emulsion is a mixture of two liquids that don't normally mix, like oil and vinegar. To emulsify oil and vinegar, add oil to vinegar slowly while whisking rapidly. This disperses and suspends the oil droplets throughout the vinegar. Emulsified mixtures are thick and creamy in texture. Mayonnaise and hollandaise are examples of emulsified mixtures.

Eggless Caesar Salad

- 1 tablespoon fresh lemon juice
- 2 anchovy fillets, minced (optional)
- 1 garlic clove, minced
- 1/2 teaspoon Dijon mustard
- 1/4 cup extra virgin olive oil
- 1 tablespoon freshly grated Parmesan cheese
- salt and freshly ground black pepper
- 1 head romaine lettuce, chopped

Whisk together lemon juice, anchovy, garlic, and mustard in a large mixing bowl.

Whisk in oil until creamy (this means the dressing is emulsified). Stir in cheese, and season to taste with salt and pepper.

Add lettuce, and toss to coat.

Turkey Sausages with Kale and Garbanzo Beans

- 1 tablespoon extra virgin olive oil
- 1 pound Italian turkey sausages, sweet or hot
- 1 small onion, diced
- 3 cloves garlic, minced
- 1 1/2 cups chicken stock
- 1 bunch kale, roughly chopped
- 1 (14-ounce) can garbanzo beans, rinsed and drained
- salt and freshly ground black pepper to taste

Heat oil in a large sauté pan over medium-high heat. Add sausages, and cook until browned on all sides, turning occasionally, about 6 minutes. Remove from pan, and slice diagonally (sausage may not be completely done).

Add onion and garlic to sauté pan, and cook over medium heat until soft, about 3 minutes. Add stock, and bring to a simmer. Add kale, cover, and cook until kale has wilted, about 5 minutes.

Add sausages, cover, and cook until no longer pink in the center, about 5 minutes. Add garbanzo beans and continue cooking, covered, until heated through, about 2 minutes. Season to taste with salt and pepper.

Asian Menu I

For a heartier version of these rolls, use rice paper in place of the lettuce leaves. Add shrimp or chicken to the rolls, or use pork instead of chicken for the curry.

Vietnamese Pork Rolls

1	tablespoon Asian fish sauce
1	tablespoon fresh lime juice
2	teaspoons minced fresh ginger
1	garlic clove, minced
	pinch red pepper flakes
1	tablespoon canola oil
1	pound pork cutlets
	salt and freshly ground black pepper
1	head Napa cabbage, shredded
1	small red bell pepper, cut into thin strips
8	large Boston lettuce leaves

For the dressing: Whisk together fish sauce, lime juice, ginger, garlic, and red pepper flakes in a small bowl.

For the pork: Heat oil in a large skillet over medium heat. Season pork with salt and pepper, and sauté until lightly browned, 3 minutes per side. Remove from heat, and slice into thin strips. Toss with 1 tablespoon of the dressing.

Combine cabbage, bell pepper, and remaining dressing in a large bowl. Lay lettuce leaves on a clean, dry work surface. Divide pork among leaves. Top with cabbage mixture and roll tightly, tucking edges in as you go. Place rolls, seam side down, on a cutting board, cut in half, and serve.

Jasmine Rice

1½	cups jasmine rice
	salt to taste

Rinse the rice once, moving your fingers through the rice, until the water runs pure, without any murkiness. Drain.

Place rice in a pot. Add enough water to cover rice by ¾ inch, about 1¾ cups water. Add a pinch of salt, and stir.

Bring rice to a boil, uncovered. Turn heat down to lowest setting. Cover and simmer until rice is cooked through, 17–19 minutes.

Simply Chicken and Coconut Milk Curry

2	tablespoons vegetable oil
1½	teaspoons black peppercorns
3	1½–inch cinnamon sticks
10	cloves
8	cardamom pods
3	dried red chili peppers
1	tablespoon grated fresh ginger
8	large bone-in, skinless chicken thighs
	14-ounce can coconut milk
	sea salt

Heat the oil in a large heavy pot over high heat. Add the peppercorns, cinnamon, cloves, cardamom, and chilies. Stir for a few minutes, until the cardamom darkens slightly. Add the ginger, and give a few stirs.

Add the chicken and coconut milk. Salt very lightly. Add enough water just to cover the chicken pieces. Bring to a boil, turn down to a simmer, and cook for 40 minutes or until the chicken is cooked through and the sauce thickens slightly. Season to taste with salt.

Asian Menu II

Use an orange instead of a lemon in the lemon chicken recipe for a different taste. For those non-seafood-eating clients of yours, replace the shrimp with more chicken or pork. Serve a store-bought sweet-and-sour sauce or hot mustard sauce with the meatballs.

Pork and Shiitake Meatballs

10	medium dried shiitake mushrooms
2	pounds ground pork
2	tablespoons soy sauce
1	teaspoon sea salt
1	teaspoon sugar
¼	cup finely chopped green onion
1	teaspoon toasted sesame oil
2	large eggs

Place the mushrooms in a bowl, and cover them with boiling water. Let stand until completely soft, about 30 minutes. Squeeze the water out of the mushrooms with your hands, remove the tough stems, and mince finely. Place in a large bowl.

Add the pork, soy sauce, salt, sugar, green onion, oil, and eggs. Mix until everything is well combined.

Bring a large pot of water to a boil. Shape the mixture into 24 meatballs, using 2 tablespoons for each. Drop the meatballs gently into the water. When the water returns to a boil, cover the pot, turn down the heat to a simmer, and cook gently for 15 minutes. Remove with a slotted spoon.

Chinese Lemon Chicken

2	pounds mixed bone-in chicken parts or chicken thighs
1	tablespoon mirin (rice wine) or rice vinegar
1	tablespoon soy sauce
1	tablespoon honey
1	lemon
1	tablespoon vegetable oil
3	slices peeled fresh ginger
1/2	teaspoon salt

If using mixed chicken parts, chop the chicken through the bone into 2-inch pieces with a meat cleaver, or disjoint into serving pieces.

In a medium bowl, combine the rice wine, soy sauce, and honey.

Slice 1/8 inch off both ends of the lemon. Halve the lemon crosswise, and cut each half into 4 wedges. Remove any visible seeds.

Heat one large skillet or two smaller ones over high heat until hot but not smoking. Add the oil, lemon wedges, and ginger, and stir-fry for 1–2 minutes or until the lemon and ginger are slightly browned. Be careful; the wet lemon wedges will cause the oil to splatter. Transfer the lemon and ginger to a small plate.

Carefully add the chicken to the skillet, skin side down, in a single layer. Fry for 3–4 minutes, adjusting the heat between medium and medium-high as the chicken browns. Using a metal spatula, turn the chicken over, and fry 3–4 minutes more, or until the chicken is browned on the other side but not cooked through. Pour off any excess fat.

Sprinkle on the salt, the wine mixture, and the lemon and ginger. Cover and simmer over medium heat for 3–4 minutes (8–10 minutes for chicken thighs). Turn the chicken, reduce the heat to low, and simmer for 3–4 minutes more (8–10 minutes for thighs) or until the chicken is cooked through. Serve immediately.

Shrimp Noodles

6	cups water
1	cup soy sauce
1	cup sake
1/2	cup mirin, sweet sherry, or sweet vermouth
12	ounces dried soba noodles
1	cup cooked fresh spinach, chopped
1	pound boneless, skinless chicken breasts, thinly sliced on the diagonal
6	jumbo shrimp, deveined but left in their shells
1	medium onion, thinly sliced
2	green onions (white and green parts), cut into 2-inch pieces
3	tablespoons fresh lemon juice
2	tablespoons Asian sesame oil
	hot chili oil to taste
1/4	cup sesame seeds, toasted, for garnish

In a large nonreactive saucepan, combine the water, soy sauce, sake, and mirin. Bring to a boil over high heat. Reduce the heat to low, and simmer to cook off the alcohol and let the flavors blend, about 30 minutes.

Meanwhile, bring a large saucepan of salted water to a boil over medium-high heat. Add the noodles, return to a boil, and cook until just tender, 2–3 minutes. Drain thoroughly in a colander. Divide the noodles and the spinach among six soup bowls.

Add the chicken, shrimp, onion, and green onions to the simmering stock, and cook until the shrimp and chicken are tender, about 10 minutes.

Remove from the heat. Add 1 shrimp to each serving of noodles and spinach, then add the chicken and vegetables, dividing them evenly. Ladle the stock into the bowls, then drizzle each serving with lemon juice, sesame oil, and chili oil. Garnish with the sesame seeds, and serve.

Mexican Menu

Tomatoes and green onion are delightful additions to this salad. Use two or three different types of Mexican cheeses for the enchiladas, like Cotija or Manchego. Canned diced green chilies are another perfect stuffer for these enchiladas.

Avocado, Jicama, and Watercress Salad

	juice of 2 limes
3	serrano chilies, or to taste, thinly sliced
1/4	teaspoon salt
	freshly ground black pepper to taste
1/2	cup extra virgin olive oil
2	cups watercress, heavy stems removed
1	jicama, peeled and cut into fine julienne
2	avocados, peeled, pitted, and sliced

Combine the lime juice, serrano chilies, salt, and pepper in a small bowl. Drizzle in the olive oil in a steady stream, whisking constantly to emulsify.

In a medium bowl, combine the watercress and jicama. Add the vinaigrette, and toss. Carefully fold in the avocado, and serve.

Chicken Enchiladas

2	cups red or green enchilada sauce
12	corn tortillas
16	ounces shredded Monterey Jack cheese
12	ounces shredded cooked chicken
1/4	cup thinly sliced green onion

Preheat oven to 350°F. Lightly grease a 9 x 13 casserole dish, and set aside.

Bring enchilada sauce to a boil, then turn down to a simmer. Dip one tortilla into the sauce for 5 seconds until it softens. Lay on a flat surface, and in the middle of the tortilla, sprinkle with 1 ounce of cheese, 1 ounce of chicken, and 1 tablespoon of green onion. Roll one side over the other, and lay seam side down in casserole dish. Repeat for remaining 11 enchiladas.

Pour remaining enchilada sauce evenly over all of the enchiladas, and sprinkle the rest of the cheese.

Cover and bake for 20 minutes, until the cheese inside the enchiladas is completely melted and chicken is warm. Uncover and cook for another 2–3 minutes, until the cheese on top is bubbling. Let cool for 5 minutes, and serve.

Green Rice

1	cup tightly packed stemmed spinach leaves
1/2	cup tightly packed cilantro sprigs
1 1/4	cups homemade or canned low-salt chicken stock
1 1/2	cups milk
1	teaspoon salt
3	tablespoons unsalted butter
1	tablespoon olive oil
1 1/2	cups long-grain white rice
1/4	cup minced onion
1	garlic clove, minced

Place the spinach, cilantro, and stock in a blender, and blend until the vegetables are pureed. Add the milk and salt, and blend until well combined.

In a medium saucepan, heat the butter and olive oil over medium heat. When the butter is melted, add the rice and sauté, stirring frequently, until it just begins to brown, 3–4 minutes. Add the onion and garlic, and cook for 1 minute, stirring constantly. Add the spinach mixture, stir well, increase the heat to high, and bring to a boil. Cover, reduce the heat to low, and cook for 20 minutes. Stir the rice carefully to avoid crushing it, cover, and cook for 5 minutes more.

Remove from the heat, and let the rice steam in the covered pot for 10 minutes. Serve hot.

Italian Menu I

To make a low-carb variation to the traditional Italian Bolognese lasagna, use thinly sliced eggplant or zucchini instead of lasagna noodles.

Sweet Onion Frittata

2	tablespoons unsalted butter
1	tablespoon olive oil
2	large sweet onions, thinly sliced
1/2	teaspoon salt
1/4	teaspoon black pepper
10	eggs
1/4	cup whole milk
1/2	cup Asiago cheese, grated
2	teaspoons fresh thyme (or 1/2 teaspoon dried thyme)

Preheat oven to 350°F. Generously grease a 10-inch pie or cake pan with 1 tablespoon of butter.

Heat oil and remaining butter in a large sauté pan over medium-high heat. Add onions, salt, and pepper, and cook until golden; about 10 minutes. Remove onions from pan and set aside.

Whisk eggs and milk together. Stir in cheese, thyme, and onions. Pour into prepared pie or cake pan, and bake until top begins to brown and eggs puff up in the center; about 15 minutes.

Bolognese Lasagna

1½	pounds ricotta cheese
2	large eggs
⅛	teaspoon freshly grated nutmeg
½	teaspoon sea salt
½	cup freshly grated Parmesan cheese
3	cups bolognese sauce or meat sauce, warm
7	ounces oven-ready lasagna noodles
1½	cups shredded mozzarella cheese

Preheat oven to 350°F. In a medium bowl, mix the ricotta, eggs, nutmeg, salt, and Parmesan. Cover, and refrigerate up to 1 day.

Spread one quarter of the sauce in a 13 x 9-inch baking dish. Carefully transfer 6 lasagna noodles to the dish. Spread with another one quarter of the sauce. Evenly spread the ricotta filling on top.

Add more sauce, the last 6 lasagna noodles, and the rest of the sauce.

Bake for 35 minutes. Sprinkle with the mozzarella, and bake 10 minutes longer. Remove from the oven, and let rest for 10 minutes before serving.

Garlic Bread

1	French baguette
¼	cup extra virgin olive oil
2	tablespoons garlic powder
2	tablespoons onion powder
2	tablespoon paprika
2	tablespoons dried parsley flakes
½	cup grated Parmesan cheese
	salt and freshly ground pepper to taste

Preheat oven to 400°F. Cut the baguette in half lengthwise. Brush 1/8 cup olive oil on one half of the bread and the remaining olive oil on the second half.

Sprinkle one half of the bread with 1 tablespoon each garlic powder, onion powder, paprika, and parsley flakes. Sprinkle the remaining tablespoon of each of the seasonings on the second half.

Sprinkle 1/4 cup Parmesan cheese on one half of the bread and the rest of the cheese on the second half. Salt and pepper to taste.

Bake on a baking sheet for 10–15 minutes until bread is golden brown, cheese is completely melted, and crust is crispy.

Italian Menu II

Escarole is a traditional Italian green vegetable that is a perfect substitute for the kale dish. To add an even more Italian flair to this dish, use Italian sausage instead of turkey sausage.

Italian Pumpkin Soup

1	sugar pumpkin or butternut squash
1/3	cup extra virgin olive oil
4	tablespoons butter
1	large onion, finely chopped
	salt to taste
6–8	cups vegetable stock
1	cup heavy cream
1/3	cup amaretto liqueur
1/3	cup amaretti cookies (without sugar on top), crushed

Preheat the oven to 450°F. Place a rack at the middle level. Line a cookie sheet with foil, grease it, and set aside.

Peel the pumpkin, or squash, and cut it into small pieces (about 1 inch). Remove and discard the seeds. Spread the pieces on the cookie sheet in a single layer and roast, stirring once, for 10–20 minutes or until almost tender.

Meanwhile, in a large pot over medium heat, heat the olive oil and butter, add the onion and a pinch of salt, and cook, stirring frequently, for about 7 minutes or until onion is totally wilted.

Add the pumpkin or squash and 4 cups of the vegetable stock to the onion mixture, and simmer over medium heat until the pumpkin or squash is completely soft, 15–20 minutes. Reduce the heat to low, and stir in the cream, amaretto, and amaretti. Remove from the heat, and let cool for 15 minutes.

Transfer the soup to a food processor and puree. Return to the pot, and stir in 2 cups of stock or more to taste. Taste and add a bit more salt, if desired.

Turkey Sausages with Kale and Chickpeas

1	tablespoon extra virgin olive oil
1	pound reduced-fat sweet or hot Italian turkey sausages
1	small onion, diced
3	cloves garlic, minced
1½	cups lower-sodium chicken stock
1	bunch kale, stems removed and roughly chopped
1	can chickpeas, rinsed and drained
	salt and freshly ground black pepper to taste

Heat oil in a large saucepan over medium-high heat. Add sausages, and cook until browned on all sides, turning occasionally, about 6 minutes. Remove from pan, and cut each sausage in half on the diagonal.

Add onion and garlic to the same saucepan, and cook over medium heat until softened and translucent, about 3 minutes. Add stock, and bring to a simmer. Add kale, cover, and cook until wilted and softened, about 8 minutes.

Add sausages and cook, covered, until no longer pink in the center, about 8 minutes. Add chickpeas and continue cooking, covered, until heated through, 2 minutes. Season to taste with salt and pepper, and serve hot, spooning any remaining cooking liquid on top.

French Menu

Classic French cooking doesn't get any more traditional than this! Substitute any fresh herb—thyme, marjoram, or chervil—in the poached chicken. For richer, sweeter carrots, use brown sugar instead of regular sugar.

Poached Chicken Breasts with Tarragon

2	cups chicken stock, or as needed
2	cups dry white wine or water, or as needed
6–7	fresh tarragon sprigs, plus fresh tarragon leaves for garnish
½	yellow onion, cut in half
1	celery stalk, cut crosswise into quarters

1	teaspoon salt
4–5	peppercorns
2–3	lemon slices
4	chicken breast halves, 8–9 ounces each, skinned and boned
2	tablespoons unsalted butter
2	tablespoons all-purpose flour
1/2	cup heavy cream

In a large sauté pan or wide saucepan that will accommodate the 4 chicken breasts without crowding, combine the chicken stock and wine or water. Add the tarragon sprigs, onion, celery, salt, peppercorns, and lemon slices. Bring to a boil, reduce the heat to low, cover, and simmer gently for 15–20 minutes to extract the flavor from the vegetables.

Remove all excess fat from the chicken breasts. Rinse the breasts, then place them in the stock, adding more stock or water if the breasts are not completely covered. Bring back just to a bare simmer (do not allow it to boil), cover (or cover partially), and poach gently until the breasts are tender and the flesh is opaque throughout when pierced with a sharp knife, 20–25 minutes.

In a heavy saucepan (preferably nonstick) over medium-low heat, melt the butter until bubbling. Stir in the flour and cook, stirring, for a few seconds. While continuously stirring to avoid lumps, quickly add 1 cup of the poaching liquid. Cook, stirring, until the mixture thickens and comes to a boil. Reduce the heat to low, and cook for 1 minute longer, stirring a couple of times. Add the cream, and stir until well blended. You should have a very smooth white sauce. Do not allow it to burn or stick.

Arrange the chicken breasts on individual plates, and spoon the sauce evenly over the top to cover completely. Garnish with tarragon leaves.

Buttered Carrots

1	pound large carrots, peeled and thinly sliced
3–4	tablespoons unsalted butter
2	tablespoons sugar
1/2	teaspoon salt
1	cup water
1	lemon
4–5	fresh mint sprigs

Put carrots into a heavy saucepan together with the butter, sugar, salt, and water. Place over medium heat, and bring to a boil. Reduce the heat to medium-low, and boil gently, uncovered, until the liquid is reduced to 1–2 tablespoons syrup, about 20–25 minutes; check the carrots occasionally to be sure they are not scorching. Transfer to a serving dish.

Remove the zest from the lemon: Using a zester or a fine-holed shredder and holding the lemon over the carrots, shred the zest (yellow part only) from the skin evenly over the carrots.

Garnish with the mint sprigs.

Coq au Vin

4	slices bacon
1–2	tablespoons olive oil
1	whole chicken, cut into 8 pieces
1	cup chopped onions
2	stalks celery, chopped
6	ounces mushrooms, sliced
4	cloves garlic, finely chopped
1½	cups dry red wine
½	cup chicken stock
1	bay leaf
6	fresh thyme sprigs, or 1 tablespoon ground
¼	cup finely minced fresh parsley
	salt and freshly ground black pepper

In a large sauté pan, fry bacon until crisp over high heat. Remove bacon from the pan, and set aside. Add olive oil to the pan. Brown chicken pieces in hot oil. Remove chicken, and set aside.

Add onions to pan. Sauté for 5–7 minutes, until browned. Add celery and mushrooms, and sauté for 7 minutes more. Add garlic, and sauté for 1 minute. Pour wine and chicken stock into pan. Raise heat to high, and scrape any bits off bottom of the pan. Remove pan from heat.

Place reserved chicken pieces in pressure-cooker pot. Pour wine-vegetable mixture over chicken. Add bay leaf and thyme. Crumble reserved bacon into cooker. Lock lid into place. Bring to pressure over high heat. Reduce heat, and cook for 10 minutes. Release pressure slowly.

Remove chicken and place on a serving platter. Discard bay leaf. Add parsley to sauce. Raise heat, and bring to a boil. Reduce heat and simmer until sauce is reduced by half, about 10 minutes. Season sauce with salt and pepper. Pour sauce over chicken pieces.

Cold-Weather Menu I

Yukon gold or fingerling potatoes are a fitting alternative to red potatoes. Or make things more interesting by using two or three types of potatoes. For a heartier version of this vegetable soup, use beef stock instead of chicken stock, or use vegetable stock for your vegetarian clients.

Winter Vegetable Soup

3	tablespoons extra virgin olive oil
½	cup finely diced celery
½	cup finely diced onion
1	tablespoon finely chopped fresh parsley
2	cloves garlic, finely minced
8	cups chicken stock or water
2	cups canned Italian plum tomatoes with juice, finely chopped
1	cup diced turnips
1	cup diced daikon radish
2	cups finely chopped green cabbage
2	cups finely chopped green kale leaves
2	large Parmesan rinds
1	bay leaf
	sea salt and freshly ground black pepper
	freshly grated Parmesan cheese

Heat the oil in a very large pot over medium heat. Add the celery, onion, parsley, and garlic, and sauté until lightly browned. Add the stock or water and tomatoes. Bring to a boil.

Add the turnips, daikon, cabbage, kale, cheese rinds, and bay leaf. Season lightly with salt. Simmer for 1 hour, or until the vegetables are very tender and the soup has thickened. (If it is too thick, add additional water or stock). Season to taste with pepper and additional salt. Remove the bay leaf and cheese rinds. Serve with cheese sprinkled on top.

Braised Brisket of Beef with Port Wine

1	center-cut beef brisket, 3½–4 pounds
3	tablespoons extra virgin olive oil or vegetable oil
2	cloves garlic, chopped
1	medium yellow onion, chopped
¾	cup chopped celery
1	pound ripe plum Roma tomatoes, cored and chopped
3	whole cloves
2	orange zest strips, each 3 inches long by 1 inch wide
1	bay leaf
4	fresh thyme sprigs
3	fresh parsley sprigs
½	teaspoon salt, or to taste
	freshly ground black pepper
1	cup port wine

Position a rack in the lower part of an oven, and heat to 350°F.

Trim any excess fat from the beef. Select a large ovenproof pot or Dutch oven that will hold the meat comfortably. Add the oil, and warm over medium-high heat. When hot, add the beef, and brown on all sides, 4–5 minutes. Transfer to a plate, and set aside. Reduce the heat to low, add the garlic and onion, and sauté until translucent, 3–4 minutes. Stir in the celery and tomatoes.

To make a bouquet garni, stick the cloves into the orange zest strips, then tie together the strips, bay leaf, thyme, and parsley with kitchen string. Add to the pot along with the salt, pepper to taste, the browned beef, and ½ cup of the port. Cover tightly, and place in the oven. Braise, basting frequently with the pan juices, until tender, 2–2½ hours. Transfer the meat to a warmed platter, cover loosely with aluminum foil, and keep warm.

Discard the bouquet garni. Rest a sieve over a bowl, and pour the pot contents into it, capturing the juices in the bowl. Transfer the vegetables in the sieve to a food processor fitted with the metal blade or to a blender. Puree until smooth.

Using a spoon, skim off the fat from the reserved juices. Return the juices and pureed vegetables to the pot, add the remaining ½ cup port, and bring to a boil. Boil for a few seconds to dispel the alcohol. Adjust the seasonings.

Slice the meat about ¼ inch thick. Spoon the sauce over the slices.

Roasted Red Potatoes

It's easy to make these potatoes along with whatever else you have in the oven. They can be cooked longer at a lower temperature or at a higher temperature for a shorter time.

2   pounds small red potatoes
2   tablespoon extra virgin olive oil
    salt and freshly ground pepper to taste
    fresh rosemary, optional

Preheat oven to 350°F. Depending on how big the potatoes are, cut them in halves or in quarters. Place in a bowl and toss with olive oil, salt and pepper, and rosemary. Spread out in a single layer on a baking sheet. Bake for 35 minutes or until golden brown.

Cold-Weather Menu II

Mix and match any of your clients' favorite root vegetables to roast. Use two or three different types of wild mushrooms for the soup. Make the honey-lemon glaze into a tri-citrus glaze by adding an orange and a lime.

Creamy Mushroom Soup

2   tablespoons unsalted butter
$1/2$ cup finely chopped celery
2   tablespoons finely chopped onion
$1/4$ pound small mushrooms, thinly sliced
$1/2$ cup chicken stock
$3/4$ cup whipping cream
    sea salt and freshly ground pepper to taste

Melt butter over medium-high heat. Add celery and onion, and cook about 3 minutes, until tender and fragrant.

Add mushrooms, and cook another 5 minutes, until soft and wilted.

Add chicken stock, bring to a boil, then let simmer for about 15 minutes. Puree or blend until the texture is smooth.

Return to stove on medium-high heat, and add whipping cream. Cook for about 5–7 minutes. Salt and pepper to taste. Serve immediately.

Baked Chicken with Honey-Lemon Glaze

1	pound white boiling onions, 1 inch in diameter
1	lemon
¼	cup light honey
3	teaspoons chopped fresh thyme
1	chicken, 3½–4 pounds, preferably free-range, cut into serving pieces
3	tablespoons unsalted butter
2	tablespoons minced shallot
	salt and freshly ground black pepper
½	cup golden raisins

Position a rack in the middle of an oven and preheat to 375°F.

Trim and cut across the root end of each onion. Peel the onions, and put into a saucepan. Add water to cover, and bring to a boil. Reduce the heat to medium-low and simmer, uncovered, for 5 minutes. Drain and set aside.

Using a zester or a fine-holed shredder and holding the lemon over a bowl, shred the zest from the lemon. Then squeeze the juice into another bowl. Measure 2 tablespoons of the juice and add to the zest. Stir in the honey and 2 teaspoons of thyme. Set aside.

Remove any excess fat from the chicken pieces. Cut each breast in half crosswise. Be sure the drumsticks and thighs are separated. Remove wing tips and discard. Rinse the chicken pieces, and pat dry with paper towels.

Select a 2½- to 3-quart baking pan that holds the chicken comfortably in one layer. Combine the butter and shallot in the pan; place in the oven for 1–2 minutes to melt the butter. Add the chicken pieces, and turn to coat well; leave the pieces skin side down. Sprinkle with salt and pepper and the remaining 1 teaspoon thyme. Bake uncovered, basting a couple of times with the pan juices, for 15 minutes.

Turn the chicken skin side up, and add the onions and raisins to the pan. Baste the chicken and onions with half of the honey-lemon mixture. Return to the oven for another 10 minutes. Baste with the remaining honey-lemon mixture, reduce the heat to 350°F, and continue to bake, basting every 7–8 minutes with the pan juices, until the chicken and onions are fork-tender and golden and the pan juices have thickened to a glaze, another 25–30 minutes. If the juices have not thickened sufficiently, transfer the chicken pieces to a plate, and boil the juices on the stove top until reduced to a glaze, 2–3 minutes. Return the chicken to the pan, and turn several times in the glaze.

Arrange the chicken and onions on a serving platter. Spoon the glaze over the top and serve.

Roasted Root Vegetables

2	carrots, cut into 1-inch-thick pieces
2	parsnips, cut into 1-inch-thick pieces
2	rutabagas, cut into 1-inch-thick pieces
2	small sweet potatoes, cut into 1-inch-thick pieces
1	celery root, cut into 1-inch-thick pieces
1	golden beet, cut into 1-inch-thick pieces
⅛	cup extra virgin olive oil
2	tablespoons fresh thyme
	salt and freshly ground pepper to taste

Preheat oven to 375°F. Place vegetables in a single layer on a baking sheet.

Brush vegetables completely with enough olive oil to cover all pieces. Sprinkle with fresh thyme and salt and pepper to taste.

Cook for about 20 minutes, and turn vegetables on baking sheet to make sure all sides get cooked evenly. Cook for another 20–25 minutes until vegetables are golden brown and semitender but not mushy.

Hot-Weather Menu I

Avocados and sun-dried tomatoes in oil are hearty additions to the light, summery salad. Customize the gazpacho to fit your clients' tastes and what's available. If you want a soupier gazpacho, simply add a cup of chicken broth, or replace the green bell pepper with roasted red or yellow bell peppers for a lovely change of taste.

Gazpacho

1	cucumber, peeled, seeded, and coarsely chopped
1	green bell pepper, coarsely chopped
1	medium sweet onion, coarsely chopped
1/3	cup fresh parsley leaves
2 1/2	pounds ripe tomatoes, peeled, seeded, and coarsely chopped
1 1/2	cups tomato juice
1/4	cup red wine vinegar, more or less to taste
3	tablespoons extra virgin olive oil
2	garlic cloves, minced
1	jalapeño, seeded and minced, optional
	salt and freshly ground pepper to taste

Lightly chop in a food processor the cucumber, bell pepper, onion, and parsley. Remove, and set aside in a large bowl.

Lightly chop the tomatoes in a food processor. Remove, and add to cucumber mixture.

Add tomato juice, vinegar, olive oil, garlic, and jalapeño to cucumber and tomato mixture. Incorporate all ingredients well. Salt and pepper to taste.

Cover and chill for at least 2 hours. Serve cold.

How to Peel a Tomato

Bring a small pot of water to a boil. Cut a shallow cross in the smooth end of the tomato. Immerse it in boiling water for 20–30 seconds. Remove with a slotted spoon, and place in a bowl of ice water. Using a paring knife or your fingers, peel off the skins. Cut in half crosswise, and carefully squeeze out the seeds. Chop into desired size.

Shrimp and Spinach Salad

1	pound medium shrimp in the shell
2⅛	teaspoons salt, or to taste
½	pound young, small green beans, trimmed
½	pound baby spinach leaves, or 1 bunch young, tender spinach
1½	tablespoons fresh lemon juice
⅓	cup extra virgin olive oil
2	teaspoons minced fresh dill
	freshly ground black pepper
1	tablespoon minced green onion, including some tender green tops

Preheat broiler.

Peel, devein, and butterfly the shrimp. Place the shrimp in a bowl, and add water to cover. Add 1 teaspoon of the salt, stir to dissolve, and let stand for 10 minutes. Drain, rinse, and drain again; dry on paper towels. Set aside.

Bring a saucepan three fourths full of water to a boil. Add the green beans and 1 teaspoon salt, and bring back to a boil. Cook until tender but still crisp, 4–5 minutes. Drain, and immediately plunge into cold water to stop the cooking. Drain again, and set aside.

Rinse the baby spinach leaves, if necessary, and dry. If using bunch spinach, pick over the leaves, discarding tough and large ones, and remove the stems. Wash and dry well. If the leaves are large, tear them into small pieces. Place the spinach in a bowl.

To make the vinaigrette: In a small bowl, combine the lemon juice and the remaining ⅛ teaspoon salt, and stir to dissolve. Add the olive oil, dill, and pepper to taste, and whisk until blended. Stir in the green onion, and set aside.

Arrange the shrimp in a small broiling pan without a rack or in a flameproof baking dish. Brush the shrimp with a little of the vinaigrette, and place under the broiler about 3 inches from the heat. Broil (grill) until the shrimp turn pink, turning once, 3–4 minutes. Remove from the broiler, and add the remaining vinaigrette and the green beans to the pan or dish. Stir to coat the shrimp and beans with the vinaigrette. Using tongs, transfer the shrimp and beans to a plate.

Pour the warm vinaigrette over the spinach, and toss quickly. Divide the spinach among individual plates, and arrange the shrimp and green beans on top. Serve at once.

Garlic Breadsticks

1	(1-pound) package frozen bread dough, thawed
1/8	cup extra virgin olive oil
2	garlic cloves, minced
1	tablespoon grated Parmesan cheese
	salt and freshly ground pepper to taste

Preheat oven to 400°F. Mix olive oil, garlic, and cheese. Set aside.

Cut dough into 12 equal pieces. Roll each piece into a 6-inch rope.

Lay dough on a lightly greased baking sheet. Brush with oil mixture. Sprinkle with salt and pepper.

Bake for 20 minutes until golden brown and crispy.

Hot-Weather Menu II

Apples, figs, pears, grapes, or nuts are all perfect pairings to serve with your cheese and bread platter. Make this turkey or chicken salad into a wonderful sandwich with whole wheat, rye, or pumpernickel bread.

Country Bread and Cheese Assortment

Gorgonzola

Gruyère

Gouda

Manchego

Vermont white cheddar

Brie

Camembert

French baguette

Walnut raisin bread

Whole wheat baguette

Focaccia

Water crackers

Oatcakes

Crostini

Choose four cheeses and two breads from the list above. Serve 1 ounce of each cheese and four pieces of bread or eight crackers for each serving.

Basic Sauce Recipes

Every personal chef should have a collection of basic sauces in his or her repertoire. Here are some no chef should be without.

Pan Sauces for Meat. A pan sauce is the perfect sauce for meats that are cooked stove top because the meat's own natural juices and flavor serve as the base of the sauce. After the meat is cooked or has been browned for further cooking, remove the meat and all but about 1 tablespoon of the fat from the pan. Add ½ cup of beef or veal broth, red wine, apple juice or white grape juice, or water to the pan over medium heat. Cook 2–3 minutes, scraping the bottom of pan to release browned bits (these give your sauce great flavor). Increase heat to high, and add another ½ cup of liquid, any herbs you want to use for flavoring, and any leftover juices from the meat. Boil and reduce for 2–4 minutes. Remove from heat, and add a table-spoon of room-temperature butter (if desired), stirring until well blended. Taste and add salt and pepper to taste. This will make about ½ cup of sauce.

Pan Sauces for Poultry. Use the same basic recipe above. For the liquid, use chicken broth, white wine, citrus juices, or water.

Basic White Sauce. Melt 2 tablespoons butter in a pan over medium heat. Stir in ¼ cup all-purpose flour, and cook for 1 minute to get rid of the raw-flour taste. Gently whisk in 1 cup milk, whisking constantly to prevent lumps. Add ½ teaspoon salt, ⅛ teaspoon ground black pepper, and ⅛ teaspoon grated nutmeg (optional). Whisk in another cup of milk until thick and bubbling. Lower heat, and simmer for 2–3 minutes until very thick and smooth.

Cheese Sauce. Follow the basic white sauce recipe above and stir in 1½ cups (6 ounces) shredded or crumbled cheese, 1 teaspoon Dijon mustard (optional), and ⅛ teaspoon ground red pepper (optional). Any soft, semisoft, or semihard cheeses work with this recipe. Cheddar, Swiss, Gruyère, Gorgonzola, and Fontina all work great. For strong-flavored cheeses, mix half and half with a more mild-flavored cheese.

Cold Sage Sauce. Combine 1 cup mayonnaise, juice from half an orange, 1 tablespoon finely chopped fresh sage, and 1 teaspoon balsamic vinegar. This sauce is ideal with poached or grilled seafood, or roasted pork or veal.

Raspberry Sauce. Mash ¼ cup fresh (or frozen and thawed) raspberries in a medium bowl. Whisk in ¼ cup raspberry or white balsamic vinegar, ½ cup walnut or light olive oil, 1 tablespoon chopped fresh tarragon, ¼ teaspoon salt, and ground black pepper to taste. This sauce is ideal to serve on grilled meats of all kinds, poached fish, or roasted chicken.

Mint-Pesto Sauce. In a food processor, place 3 garlic cloves (if you don't want the strong taste of raw garlic, chop cloves and sauté for a few minutes before adding), ¼ cup toasted almonds, and 2 cups fresh mint leaves, and process for a few seconds until everything is finely chopped. Add ½ cup extra virgin olive oil and 1 tablespoon (or more to taste) lemon juice. Process until mixture is nearly smooth. This sauce is wonderful with fish, seafood, chicken, lamb, or on vegetables.

Turkey Salad with Pistachios and Grapes

1½	pounds roast turkey or chicken, cut into ½-inch cubes
4	celery stalks, chopped
¾	cup grapes, sliced in half
⅓	cup shelled salted pistachios, roughly chopped
⅓	cup mayonnaise
¼	teaspoon salt
¼	teaspoon freshly ground black pepper

Combine turkey, celery, grapes, pistachios, mayonnaise, salt, and pepper in a large mixing bowl. Stir well to coat, and refrigerate until ready to serve.

Upscale Menu I

This is the perfect menu for those high-end clients of yours! Asparagus and Brussels sprouts are both wonderful substitutions for haricots verts. If your client is not a salmon fan, use this tasty balsamic glaze to top any firm-fleshed fresh fish, like mahi mahi or halibut.

Tomato-Leek Soup with Dill

- 2   medium leeks
- 3   tablespoons extra virgin olive oil or vegetable oil
- 2   cloves garlic, coarsely chopped
- 2   tablespoons water
- 2   pounds ripe plum Roma tomatoes, cored and coarsely chopped
- 1   medium potato, preferably baking variety, peeled and coarsely chopped
- 1   tablespoon chopped fresh dill, plus chopped fresh dill for garnish
- $\frac{1}{2}$ teaspoon salt
- $\frac{1}{8}$ teaspoon red pepper flakes
- $\frac{1}{2}$ cup sour cream
-    juice from $\frac{1}{2}$ lemon

Trim the leeks, leaving some of the tender green tops intact. Make a lengthwise slit along each leek to within about 2 inches of the root end. Place under running water to wash away any dirt lodged in between the leaves. Cut crosswise into slices $\frac{1}{2}$ inch thick. You should have about 2 cups. Set aside.

In a large saucepan over low heat, warm the oil. Add the garlic, and sauté gently for 2 minutes. Add the leeks, raise the heat to medium, and sauté, stirring until soft, 3–4 minutes. Add the water, stir, cover, and cook over medium-low heat for 4–5 minutes longer. Do not allow to boil dry; add water as necessary.

Add the tomatoes, potato, the 1 tablespoon dill, salt, and red pepper flakes to the pan. Cook uncovered over medium heat, stirring constantly, until the juices start to release, 2–3 minutes. Then cover and cook, stirring occasionally, until the tomatoes are soft and the leeks and potato are tender when pierced with a fork, 15–20 minutes longer.

Remove from heat. Pass the soup through a food mill. Fit the food mill with the medium disk, and rest the mill over a large bowl. Ladle the soup solids and liquids into the mill, and turn the handle to puree. Add lemon juice to taste.

Ladle the soup into warmed individual bowls. Float 2 tablespoons sour cream on top of each serving. Garnish with chopped dill.

Balsamic Glazed Salmon

- 4   6-ounce salmon fillets
- 1   cup balsamic vinegar
- 2   teaspoons extra virgin olive oil
- 1   teaspoon fresh lemon juice
-    salt and freshly ground black pepper

Season salmon with salt and pepper; place in an ovenproof baking dish, and bake until opaque throughout, 10–12 minutes.

While fish is cooking, place vinegar in a small saucepan. Cook over medium-high heat, stirring frequently, until reduced to $1/_3$ cup, 8–10 minutes. Remove from heat, whisk in oil and lemon juice, and season with salt and pepper. Place salmon on serving plates and drizzle with glaze.

Haricots Verts
    1   pound haricots verts, root ends trimmed
    3   tablespoons extra virgin olive oil
    1   whole shallot
         salt and freshly ground pepper to taste

Fill a pot with enough water to cover the haricots verts, and add a pinch of salt. Bring to a boil.

Place haricots verts in boiling water, and cook for about 3 minutes, just until semitender but still crunchy. Drain under cold water.

In a sauté pan over medium heat, add the olive oil. Once pan is hot, add the shallots, and cook for 2 minutes, until tender and fragrant. Add the haricots verts, and toss in the pan with the olive oil and shallots. Cook briefly for 2 minutes, until the haricots verts are hot again. Salt and pepper to taste.

Upscale Menu II
This stuffed chicken could also be made with pork chops. If goat cheese is too strong for your clients, use feta or Cotija instead. Dress up this basic rice pilaf by adding any of your clients' favorite fresh herbs, peanuts, or dried diced fruits.

Stuffed Chicken Breasts with Spinach and Goat Cheese
    4   teaspoons extra virgin olive oil, divided
    2   cloves garlic, minced
    1    $1/_2$-pound bunch spinach, tough stems removed
    4   6-ounce boneless, skinless chicken breasts
    4   ounces low-fat goat cheese
         salt and freshly ground black pepper

Saucy Tips

Sauces can be tricky things to work with. They break, they curdle, they turn strange colors. Here are some tips for rescuing your problem sauces.

- To thicken a sauce, simmer over medium to high heat until liquid reduces to the consistency you want. This concentrates and enriches the flavors. You can also add a thickener of flour, cornstarch, or arrowroot whisked into a small amount of cold water or broth. Cook until the raw taste of the flour has disappeared. To thin a sauce that is too thick, whisk more liquid into the sauce.

- Using cast-iron or noncoated aluminum pans with wine-based sauces will result in off flavors.

- Yogurt or sour cream needs to be brought to room temperature before adding to a sauce. Do not boil these sauces; they could curdle. If your sauce does curdle, remove it from the heat and whisk rapidly.

- To save a burning sauce, move sauce to another saucepan, being careful not to transfer any burnt or scorched bits (pour through a fine mesh strainer if the burnt bits are numerous). Continue cooking as if nothing untoward happened.

- If your sauce turns lumpy, puree in a blender, or press through a fine mesh sieve.

- If your sauce has a layer of fat on top, skim fat off by tilting the pan and spooning out the fat. Or put an ice cube in a slotted spoon and drag it through the surface of the sauce. The ice acts as a magnet for the fat. Discard ice cubes before they melt in the sauce.

- Avoid oversalting a sauce by adding the salt after the sauce has reduced and reached the desired consistency.

- If using purchased broth for your sauce, always use a low-sodium item. If the sauce is just a little too salty, add a pinch of sugar to balance the flavor.

- If your sauce is more than a little too salty, add water to dilute it. You can also add raw potato slices to absorb excess salt. Cook until sauce has the desired taste, then discard potatoes. This technique is not for clear sauces because the starch from the potatoes will make a clear sauce cloudy.

- To get the maximum flavor from vegetables, giblets, or herbs, chop them finely before adding them to the sauce. Pour sauce through a fine mesh strainer before finishing.

- Pureeing leftover vegetables, soups, and stews makes perfect bases for sauces.

- To flavor savory sauces, substitute nontraditional herbs and spices for traditional ones. For example, white sauces and cheese sauces generally call for grated nutmeg. To enhance the flavor use a pinch of cardamom instead.

Heat oven to 400°F.

Heat 2 teaspoons of the oil in a large ovenproof skillet over medium heat. Add garlic and cook, stirring constantly, until fragrant, about 30 seconds. Stir in spinach and cook, stirring constantly, until spinach is wilted and liquid evaporates, about 2 minutes. Season well with salt and pepper, and transfer to a plate. Wipe skillet dry with paper towels.

Beginning at the thickest end of one chicken breast, carefully insert a sharp knife into center, and cut a pocket as evenly as possible, leaving a 1-inch border on three sides. Repeat with remaining breasts. Open each pocket, sprinkle with salt and pepper, then fill evenly with goat cheese and spinach. Seal each with two toothpicks, and season outside with salt and pepper.

Heat remaining oil in the same skillet over medium-high heat. Add chicken and cook, turning once, until well browned on both sides, about 3 minutes per side. Transfer the skillet to the oven, and bake until juices run clear, about 8 minutes. Serve hot.

Rice Pilaf with Pistachios and Golden Raisins
2	tablespoons butter
1/2	cup onions, small dice
1	cup white basmati rice
2	cups low-sodium chicken broth or water
	salt and freshly ground pepper to taste
1/4	cup pistachios, finely chopped
1/4	cup golden raisins

Melt butter over medium heat. Add onions, and cook for about 3 minutes, until tender and fragrant.

Add rice, and cook for another 3 minutes, until all grains are transparent and totally coated in butter. Stir continuously.

Add chicken broth or water, salt, and pepper, and bring to a boil. Cover, then bring down to a simmer on low to medium heat. Cook for about 15 minutes until rice is tender and all of the liquid is absorbed.

Let stand covered about 5 minutes. Add pistachios and raisins.

Lemon Butter Broccolini

1	pound broccolini
2	ounces butter
2	tablespoons juice from a lemon
2	tablespoons lemon zest, minced
	salt and freshly ground pepper to taste

Fill a pot with enough water to cover the broccolini, and add a pinch of salt. Bring to a boil.

Add broccolini, and cook about 3 minutes until semitender but still crunchy. Drain under cold water.

In a pan over medium heat, melt butter. Add lemon juice and lemon zest, and cook for 1 minute, continuing to stir.

Add broccolini, and toss in pan with lemon butter mixture until broccolini is hot again. Salt and pepper to taste.

Vegetarian Menu

Use any assorted vegetables, herbs, and cheeses in the timbale to tickle your clients' taste buds. Change the pesto by adding different fresh herbs or by using pine nuts, walnuts, or other favorite nuts.

Zucchini Soup

1½–2	pounds small zucchini, grated (about 6 cups)
	salt to taste
2	tablespoons butter
2	medium yellow onions, diced
2	cups vegetable stock

freshly grated nutmeg

2   teaspoons fresh mint, chopped

3   cups milk
     freshly ground black pepper

1/2 teaspoon fresh lemon juice, or more to taste

1   teaspoon lemon zest

Spread grated zucchini over paper towels four layers thick. Sprinkle lightly with salt. Let sit for 25–30 minutes. Place paper towels on top, and squeeze out liquid.

Rinse zucchini under cold running water. Place on fresh paper towels, and squeeze out excess water. Set aside.

Melt butter in a large saucepan over medium-low heat. Add onion, and sauté until translucent, about 4 minutes. Add stock, cover, and simmer until onion is tender, about 15 minutes. Pour into the work bowl of a food processor, and pulse until smooth.

Return onion puree to pan. Add zucchini, pinch of nutmeg, and 1 teaspoon of mint. Bring to a boil, cover, reduce heat, and simmer for 7 minutes. Add milk, and season with salt, pepper, and lemon juice. Cook until heated through. Do not boil. Remove from heat, and stir in remaining mint and lemon zest.

Spaghetti with Pesto

1   cup fresh flat-leaf parsley

1   cup fresh basil

1   cup fresh mint
     leaves from 1 sprig fresh sage
     leaves from 1 sprig fresh thyme
     leaves from 1 sprig fresh rosemary

2   cloves garlic

1   cup extra virgin olive oil

1   teaspoon sugar

3/4 cup almonds

2   tablespoons freshly grated pecorino cheese
     salt and freshly ground black pepper to taste

1   pound dried spaghetti or linguini

8   plum tomatoes, diced

In a food processor, puree herbs, garlic, and oil. Add sugar and almonds, and process until almonds are coarsely ground. Add cheese, and process until mixture is the consistency of thick paste. Add salt and pepper to taste. Transfer to a large bowl.

Bring a large pot of salted water to a boil. Add the pasta, and cook according to package instructions.

Add a half cup of pasta cooking water and tomatoes to pesto. Stir to combine. Drain pasta, pour into bowl with pesto, and toss.

Vegetarian Timbale

- 5 ounces broccoli florets, sliced into ¼-inch-thick slices
- 4 ounces green beans, sliced diagonally into ¼-inch-thick slices
- ¼ cup all-purpose flour
- ½ teaspoon salt
- ¼ teaspoon freshly ground black pepper
- 2 medium zucchini, cut lengthwise into ¼-inch-thick slices
- 1 large eggplant, cut lengthwise into ¼-inch-thick slices
- 4 large eggs, lightly beaten
  canola or vegetable oil for frying
- 3 cups tomato sauce
- 7 ounces shredded Fontina or Gruyère cheese
- 1 cup freshly grated Parmesan cheese

Preheat oven to 400°F. Bring a large pot of salted water to a boil. Cook broccoli and green beans until just tender, about 1 minute. Rinse under cold running water, and drain. Pat dry with paper towels.

Place flour in a small bowl, and season with salt and pepper. Dust zucchini, eggplant, broccoli, and green beans with flour mixture, shaking off excess.

Dip in beaten egg.

In a large skillet, heat 1 inch of oil to 375°F. Fry vegetables in batches until golden brown on both sides, about 5 minutes. Drain on paper towels.

Spread 1/4 cup of tomato sauce in a 2-quart baking dish. Layer half the eggplant, Fontina or Gruyère, a third of the remaining tomato sauce, a third of the Parmesan, and half the green beans, zucchini, and broccoli in baking dish. Repeat layers, ending with a layer of tomato sauce and Parmesan.

Bake for 30 minutes, or until golden brown.

Vegan Menu

Make the curried seitan different every time by using red, yellow, or green curry. Change the shape or even grind it up. Using half red peppers and half yellow peppers will sweeten the soup. Add broccoli to the cauliflower for variety.

About Timbales

A timbale is a savory custard of heavy cream and eggs that traditionally includes grains, meats, or seafood. It is typically cooked in a small, individual drum-shaped mold and then inverted and unmolded right before serving. A vegetable timbale is the most common type and can be served with Madeira, marinara, or Mornay sauce, or any type of sauce you wish. Vegetable timbales can be a mixture of spinach, broccoli, asparagus, mushrooms, tomatoes, cauliflower, zucchini, corn, onions, and shallots. Adding fresh bread crumbs to your timbale will make it heartier and give you a less custardlike texture. Swiss, cheddar, or Parmesan cheese is baked in the timbale and is usually sprinkled on top for added flavor.

Rich Red Pepper Soup

2	tablespoons olive oil
8	large red bell peppers, roasted, seeded, and coarsely chopped
3	carrots, peeled and cut into 1/4-inch-thick slices
3	shallots, chopped
2	cloves garlic, chopped
4	cups vegetable stock
1	ripe pear, peeled and chopped
1	teaspoon salt
	pinch cayenne pepper
1/3	cup orange juice (optional)
	soy sour cream or plain soy yogurt for garnish (optional)
	fresh cilantro leaves, chopped

Heat oil in a large sauté pan over medium heat. Add bell peppers, carrots, shallots, and garlic. Cover and cook for about 15 minutes, stirring occasionally, until the vegetables are soft but not browned. Add the stock and pear, and simmer for 20–30 minutes, or until the vegetables are tender. Remove from heat and let cool.

Puree soup and season to taste with salt and cayenne pepper. Thin soup with orange juice if necessary. Can be served hot, cold, or at room temperature. Garnish with soy sour cream or soy yogurt and cilantro.

Fabulous Flavor Booster: Roasted Peppers

Roasting is a great way to boost flavor in just about any recipe that requires peppers. It's quick and easy to do, too. Simply turn a gas burner on high, and place the whole pepper directly on top of the flame. Using tongs, turn peppers frequently until skin is black and blistered. Place in a bowl, and sprinkle lightly with salt and pepper. Cover tightly with plastic wrap and let sit for 15–20 minutes. Peel off skin and remove seeds, membranes, and stem under gently running water. Use right away, or cut into large strips, drizzle with olive oil, and store in an airtight container.

Curried Seitan with Basmati Rice

1	pound seitan
2	tablespoons plus 1 teaspoon fresh lime juice
1³/₄	cups water
¹/₂	teaspoon salt
1	cup basmati rice, rinsed
2	Earth Balance or other vegan margarine
2	tablespoons extra virgin olive oil
	freshly ground black pepper
1	medium yellow onion, diced
2–3	tablespoons curry powder, to taste
¹/₂	cup vegetable stock
1	cup coconut milk
1	tablespoon fresh dill, chopped

Slice seitan into 1-inch-wide strips. Place in a medium bowl, and toss with 2 tablespoons lime juice. Set aside for 15 minutes.

What Is Seitan?

Seitan is a nonfat protein- and iron-rich Asian meat substitute made with wheat instead of soy, which is why it is also known as *wheat gluten* or *wheat meat*. Seitan is ideal for vegan diets because it gives added texture and protein. Seitan is available as a packaged mix or ready-to-use in a jar or tub. It is commonly sold in the liquid it was cooked in, which you can flavor with soy sauce and ginger or with Mexican, Italian, Thai, or other various seasonings.

Cutlets or small chunks can be pan-fried or lightly battered and deep-fried. Thin slices can be simmered in a sauce. You can grind it in a food processor or meat grinder and use it just as you would ground meat.

Seitan should be cooked only as long as it takes to heat through. It should be sauced thoroughly to hide the somewhat bitter taste.

Combine water and $\frac{1}{2}$ teaspoon salt in a saucepan. Bring to a boil. Add rice and reduce heat to low, cover, and cook 15 minutes. Remove from heat, and let stand 5 minutes.

Blot seitan pieces dry on paper towels. Place 1 tablespoon Earth Balance and 1 tablespoon olive oil in a large sauté pan over medium-high heat. When hot, add half the seitan, season with salt and pepper, and sauté until golden. Transfer seitan to a plate, and add the remaining Earth Balance and oil to pan. Add remaining seitan, season with salt and pepper, and cook until golden. Transfer seitan to plate.

Turn heat to low. Add onion, and cook for 1 minute. Stir in curry powder, and cook for 2 minutes longer. Stir in vegetable stock, scraping up any browned bits stuck to the bottom. Cover, and simmer over low heat for 5–6 minutes.

Stir in coconut milk and continue to cook, uncovered, until slightly thickened, about 2 minutes. Stir in remaining lime juice. Add salt and pepper to taste. Return seitan to pan; stir to coat well. Cook until just heated through.

Toss rice with dill.

Cauliflower with Cherry Tomatoes

	florets from 1 head cauliflower
2	tablespoons Earth Balance or other vegan margarine
$\frac{1}{2}$	medium yellow onion, chopped
2	tablespoons water
1	fresh green Anaheim chili, sliced
$\frac{3}{4}$	pound cherry tomatoes, cut in half
	salt and freshly ground black pepper
2	teaspoons fresh cilantro, chopped

Bring a saucepan three fourths full of water to a boil. Add cauliflower, reduce heat, and simmer until just tender, about 4 minutes. Drain and set aside.

Meanwhile, melt Earth Balance in a sauté pan over medium-low heat. Add onion, and sauté for 1 minute. Add 1 tablespoon of the water, cover, and cook until onion is translucent, about 3 minutes. Add chili slices and remaining water, cover, and cook for another 3 minutes.

Add tomatoes. Sauté until tomatoes begin to break down, about 2 minutes. Add salt and pepper to taste. Remove from heat.

Stir in cauliflower and cilantro.

Four Simple Sauces for Steamed Vegetables

Dijon-Walnut Sauce. In a small bowl whisk together 2 tablespoons walnut oil, 3 tablespoons red wine vinegar, 3 tablespoons tea, 2 teaspoons Dijon mustard, ¼ teaspoon salt, and ¼ teaspoon ground black pepper. Stir in 1 tablespoon toasted chopped walnuts.

Creamy Goat Cheese Sauce. In a blender or food processor, combine ⅓ cup buttermilk or low-fat plain yogurt, 2 ounces mild goat cheese, 2 teaspoons olive oil, ¼ teaspoon dried thyme, ¼ teaspoon ground black pepper, and ½ of a crushed fresh garlic clove. Blend until the mixture is smooth.

Sesame-Orange Sauce. In a small saucepan over medium-high heat, combine 1 cup orange juice, 2 large chopped shallots, 1 tablespoon red wine vinegar, 1½ teaspoons grated orange zest, and 1½ teaspoons soy sauce. Cook until liquid reduces to ½ cup, about 5 minutes. Stir in 1 teaspoon toasted sesame oil and 1 teaspoon toasted sesame seeds.

Rosemary-Garlic Sauce. Flatten 1 garlic clove on a cutting board with the broad side of a knife. Sprinkle with ½ teaspoon of kosher salt, and mash to a paste. Place mixture in a small bowl, and add 2 tablespoons olive oil, 2 tablespoons red wine vinegar, 2 tablespoons apple juice, 2 teaspoons chopped fresh rosemary, 2 teaspoons Dijon mustard, ½ teaspoon anchovy paste, and ½ teaspoon ground black pepper. Whisk mixture until smooth.

Appendix A:
A Brief Culinary Dictionary

I include this to help you understand culinary terminology and write better recipes to dazzle your clients.

Aioli: A mayonnaise primarily flavored with garlic and popular with fish, meats, and vegetables. It originates from the Provence region of southern France.

A la carte: Menu terminology that means that each item is priced individually.

Al dente: In Italian, this phrase translates as "to the tooth," which means to cook not soft or overdone. This usually refers to pasta and vegetables that are cooked until slightly crunchy and not completely tender.

Amaranth: A nourishing high-protein food that is slightly sweet in flavor; it can be used in salads and regular cooking. The nutritious amaranth seed can either be used for cereal or ground into flour for bread.

Ancho chili: This rich and slightly fruit-flavored chili is the dried version of a fresh green poblano chili. It is deep red and brown in color and ranges in hotness and flavor from mild to strong.

Andouille sausage: A traditional Cajun smoked sausage typically used in jambalaya and gumbo. It is heavy in spice and made from pork chitterlings and tripe.

Anise: The anise leaf and seed are used in both baking and cooking and impart a distinct, sweet licorice flavor. It is a member of the parsley family.

Arborio rice: A high-starch grain grown in Italy that is traditionally used for risotto because of the creamy texture it creates as it cooks.

Aromatic: Any type of herb, spice, or plant that lends flavor and fragrance to food and drinks.

Aspic: A clear or opaque savory jelly composed of gelatin and clarified meat, fish, or vegetable stock.

Au jus: A phrase commonly used with beef, which translates as meat served with its own natural juices.

Baguette: A long, narrow French loaf of bread with a crisp brown crust and a light, chewy inside.

Baking powder: A leavener that when mixed with liquid releases carbon dioxide gas bubbles that enable bread or cake to rise. It is composed of baking soda, an acid, and a moisture absorber. For a longer shelf life, keep it in a cool, dry place.

Baking soda: A leavener that when mixed with an acid, such as yogurt or buttermilk, produces carbon dioxide gas bubbles that enable a dough or batter to rise. Always mix with dry ingredients first before adding liquid because it reacts immediately when moistened.

Basil: A member of the mint family, basil is most often leafy and green but can also be purple. Basil has a combination licorice and clove flavor. It is the primary ingredient in Italian pesto.

Basmati rice: A long-grained, fine-textured rice that has a fragrant, nutlike flavor and aroma. It is aged to decrease its moisture content.

Baste: To continuously spoon or brush food with liquid such as stock, meat juice, wine, melted butter, or fat while it is cooking to ensure maximum color, flavor, and moisture.

Bay leaf: An aromatic herb that comes from the evergreen bay laurel tree used to flavor stews, soups, vegetables, and meats. Dry leaves are more available than fresh leaves and impart less flavor to a dish. Too many bay leaves may give a bitter flavor. Remove before serving.

Béarnaise sauce: A traditional French sauce that accompanies meat, fish, eggs, and vegetables. It is composed of egg yolks, butter, wine, a vinegar reduction, tarragon, and shallots.

Béchamel sauce: A basic French white sauce that is made by adding milk into a roux of butter and flour. The proportion of the roux to the milk determines the thickness of the sauce.

Beurre blanc: A classic French sauce that pairs well with poultry, seafood, vegetables, and eggs. Literally meaning "white butter," it is composed of a wine, vinegar, and shallot reduction that has chunks of cold butter gradually whisked into it until desired thickness and taste is reached.

Bind: To thicken something by stirring a variety of ingredients, such as dairy or flour, into a hot liquid.

Bisque: A hearty, rich soup composed of cream and pureed seafood or sometimes fowl or vegetables.

Blackened: A style of Cajun cooking that typically consists of a piece of meat or fish rubbed in Cajun spices and cooked in a flaming hot cast-iron skillet to allow for an extra crisp, dark, and flavorful crust.

Blanch: A cooking technique of briefly adding food, most often vegetables and fruit, to boiling water and immediately shocking them in cold water to stop them from further cooking. This allows for maximum color and flavor, firm texture, and loose skin.

Boil: To bring liquid to a temperature of 212°F or until bubbles break the liquid surface.

Bolognese: A dish consisting of a hearty, thick meat and vegetable sauce intensified with wine and milk or cream for desired flavor and thickness.

Bordelaise sauce: A classic French sauce most often served with broiled meats. It is composed of red or white wine, brown stock, bone marrow, shallots, parsley, and herbs.

Bouillon: The liquid that is strained off after cooking vegetables, poultry, meat, or fish in water, which can be used for the base of soups and sauces.

Bouquet garni: The classic trio of parsley, thyme, and bay leaf either tied together or wrapped in cheesecloth and used to flavor stews, soups, and broths.

Braise: A long, slow cooking method that requires meat or vegetables first to be browned in fat, then cooked, tightly covered in a small amount of liquid at low heat for a long period of time, either on the stove top or in the oven. This allows the food to become more flavorful as well as tender by breaking down its fibers.

Broil: To cook food in an oven directly under the gas or electric heat source or to cook food on a barbecue grill directly over the charcoal or other heat source.

Cajun seasoning: A bold seasoning blend characteristic of Cajun cooking that generally includes garlic, onion, chilies, black pepper, mustard, and celery. Spicier versions may include cayenne pepper.

Caraway seed: An aromatic seed that comes from the parsley family and has a nutty, slight anise flavor. It can be used in both savory and sweet cooking.

Cardamom: An aromatic spice that is a member of the ginger family and consists of a seed within a pod. Whether used whole, ground, or just the seed alone, the flavor is warm, spicy-sweet, and very pungent.

Cayenne pepper: Also called red pepper, it is a hot, pungent powder made from various tropical chilies that include the bright red, extremely hot cayenne pepper.

Cheesecloth: A natural fine or coarse woven cotton cloth that has various jobs in the kitchen, including straining liquids and forming bags for herbs and spices (like the bouquet garni that are used in soups, stews, and stocks).

Chervil: An aromatic herb that is a member of the parsley family; it has the delicate, light flavor of anise. Chervil has curly, dark leaves and tends to lose its flavor when dried or boiled.

Chiffonade: A culinary term used to describe herbs or vegetables that are sliced or shredded very thinly and either lightly cooked or used raw for garnishes of certain dishes, like soups.

Chili powder: A powdered blend of herbs and spices that consists of dried chilies, oregano, coriander, cumin, cloves, and garlic.

Chinois: A metal sieve shaped like a cone used for straining and pureeing. It has a mesh so fine that a tool, such as the bowl of a ladle, is typically used to force the ingredients through the mesh. Chinois is French for "China cap."

Chipotle chili: A dried, smoked jalapeño used in many stews and sauces that has a smoky, spicy, yet sweet flavor. It has a dark brown color and can be dried, pickled, and canned in adobo sauce.

Chive: A fragrant herb related to the onion and leek that has a bright green, thin, hollow stem. Because their onion flavor is mild, chives are often either used fresh or added at the end of the cooking time of a dish.

Choron sauce: The classic French sauce of hollandaise or béarnaise with the addition of tomato puree. It is typically served with poultry, meat, or fish.

Chutney: A spicy condiment that can be either chunky or smooth in texture and either hot or mild in flavor. It usually consists of fruit, sugar, spices, and vinegar.

Cilantro: Also called Chinese parsley and coriander, it is the bright green leaf and stem of the coriander plant. It is mostly used in spicy foods because of its distinct, fresh, and lively flavor.

Clarified butter: Unsalted butter that has been slowly melted over low heat to cause the milk solids to separate and form just the golden liquid left on the surface. This golden liquid is used in cooking and flavoring foods.

Clove: A dried spice that comes from the unopened flower bud of the tropical ever-green clove tree. Cloves are either whole, nail-shaped, or ground and are used in both savory and sweet dishes.

Compound butter: Butter that is softened and creamed with the addition of herbs and spices such as garlic, parsley, chives, shallots, or wine. It is mostly used as a spread or a filling, but it can also be used to cook with.

Confit: Meat that is first preserved then cooked in its own fat. Duck and goose are the two most common types of confit.

Consommé: A meat or fish broth or stock that has been clarified. It is typically served plain as a hot or cold soup but can also be used as the base of a soup or sauce.

Coriander: Related to the parsley family, the coriander plant provides the bright green leaves and stems otherwise known as cilantro or Chinese parsley. It has a flavor combination of lemon, sage, and caraway.

Cornstarch: A dense powder commonly used to thicken sauces, soups, puddings, and other foods. To prevent lumping while cooking and a starchy aftertaste to food, first add the cornstarch to a small amount of cold water to form a paste, then add it to the food.

Coulis: Generally referred to as a thick puree or sauce, such as a red bell pepper coulis or a tomato coulis.

Cream sauce: A classic French béchamel sauce that is made with milk or sometimes cream for richer foods. It can be used as the base of a dish or just as a sauce.

Cumin: The dried fruit of a plant from the parsley family that can either be used as a seed or ground. It has a nutty flavor and is a component of many curries and chili powders.

Curry: Typically refers to a hot, spicy, gravy-based East Indian dish in which curry powder is the main component. Curry powder is a blend of more than twenty different herbs, spices, and seeds that include chilies, cinnamon, cloves, cardamom, coriander, cumin, mace, nutmeg, red and black pepper, fenugreek, fennel seed, poppy seed, sesame seed, saffron, tamarind, and turmeric. There are numerous blends of curry powder.

Deglaze: Adding liquid to a pan over heat to loosen small, brown bits and particles left over from cooking or browning meat or fish. The liquid is often wine or stock and is then ultimately used as the base of a sauce to accompany what was just previously cooked in that pan.

Degrease: Using a spoon to skim off fat or layers of grease from the top of a hot liquid, such as soups, stocks, sauces, and gravies.

Dill: A feathery green-leaf herb that is most flavorful in its fresh, raw form rather than dried or cooked. Dill seed is another form of dill and gives off an even more pungent flavor when cooked.

Emulsifier: A binding ingredient used to bring together two liquids that cannot otherwise be naturally combined on their own. It can also be an ingredient used to thicken and bind sauces like hollandaise.

Emulsion: A mixture in which one liquid cannot combine with another liquid on its own, such as oil and water. It needs an emulsifier, like an egg, or rapid whisking to bring the two liquids together.

Fennel: An aromatic plant that tastes like licorice. It comes whole as a vegetable or in seed form as a spice and is used in sweet and savory dishes.

Five-spice powder: Also known as Chinese five spice, this is a mixture made up of cinnamon, cloves, fennel seed, star anise, and Szechwan peppercorns. It is primarily used in Chinese cuisine.

Fumet: A fish or mushroom stock that is concentrated and used to add flavor to other stocks and sauces.

Garam masala: An Indian spice made up of black pepper, cinnamon, cloves, coriander, cumin, cardamom, dried chilies, fennel, mace, nutmeg, and various other spices, which is primarily used in Indian cuisine.

Ginger: A slightly peppery and sweet spice that comes fresh whole, dried ground, candied, preserved, and pickled. It is typically used in Jamaican, Indian, African, and Chinese cuisine.

Glaze: A thin, glossy substance used to coat sweet and savory foods. It gives a smooth, shiny texture, taste, and look to hot and cold foods.

Gravy: A sauce typically made of meat juices combined with wine, milk, or chicken or beef broth. It is thickened with flour, cornstarch, or other thickening agents.

Herbes de Provence: A mixture of herbs from southern France that is commonly made up of basil, fennel seed, lavender, marjoram, rosemary, sage, summer savory, and thyme. It is mostly used to season meat and vegetable dishes.

Hollandaise sauce: A creamy sauce made of butter, egg yolks, and lemon juice typically used to accompany eggs Benedict and other ingredients, such as vegetables and fish.

Hummus: A Middle Eastern sauce made of pureed chickpeas, lemon juice, garlic, and olive oil or sesame oil. It is thick in texture and is mostly used as a dip or spread for pita and other breads.

Jerk seasoning: A Jamaican blend made of chilies, thyme, cinnamon, ginger, allspice, cloves, garlic, and onion. It is used as a marinade or rub to season chicken and other grilled meats.

Leek: A vegetable related to the garlic and onion that has a softer flavor and is mostly used in soups and salads.

Lemongrass: An herb with a fragrant sour lemon flavor primarily used in Thai cuisine that comes either fresh or dried.

Louis sauce: A sauce used to accompany crab or other seafood that is made of mayonnaise, chili sauce, cream, scallions, green peppers, lemon juice, and various seasonings.

Lyonnaise sauce: A classic French sauce served with meats that is made of white wine, sautéed onions, and demi-glace.

Maltaise sauce: Hollandaise sauce that has orange juice and orange zest added to it. It usually accompanies cooked vegetables, such as asparagus and green beans.

Marinade: A liquid that typically consists of lemon juice, vinegar, or wine and herbs and spices. It is used to soak meats, fish, and vegetables for flavor and sometimes to tenderize tough meats.

Marinara: A classic Italian tomato sauce made with onions, garlic, and oregano used to accompany pastas and meats.

Marjoram: An herb from the mint family that has a sweet, mild flavor almost similar to oregano; it comes fresh and dried. Marjoram is typically served with vegetables and meats, such as veal and lamb, and should be added toward the end of the cooking process because of its light flavor.

Medallion: A piece of meat such as beef, veal, pork, or chicken that is cut in the shape of a coin.

Mirepoix: The combination of onion, celery, and carrots primarily used to flavor stocks, sauces, gravies, soups, stews, and braised foods. The ratio for stocks is 50 percent onion, 25 percent celery, and 25 percent carrot.

Monosodium glutamate: Also known as MSG, this white crystalline powder is one of the twenty-two amino acids and is used to enhance the flavor of savory foods. It is typically popular among Japanese and Chinese cuisines.

Mornay sauce: A béchamel sauce that has cheese such as Parmesan or Swiss added to it and is served with eggs, seafood, vegetables, or chicken. Fish or chicken stock, cream, or egg yolks can also be added to the sauce for extra flavor and creaminess.

Mustard: In addition to its liquid form, mustard also comes in ground and seed form. It is frequently used for flavoring meats, vegetables, salad dressings, marinades, and rubs.

Nutmeg: A spice that is warm and sweet, yet pungent, which comes whole and ground. It is used to flavor sweet and savory foods such as custards, white sauces, potatoes, and vegetables.

Oregano: An herb from the mint family that is an unsweetened yet stronger version of marjoram. It comes fresh and dried and is ideal in tomato-based dishes because of its Mediterranean origin.

Organic: Food and ingredients referred to as not having any added chemicals, fertilizers, insecticides, additives, or artificial colorings or flavors.

Panko: A coarse bread crumb typically used to coat foods to give them a crunchy texture. It is most common in Japan for coating fried foods.

Parsley: An herb with a slight peppery flavor that comes fresh and dried. It has more than thirty varieties in its family and is also used as a classic garnish.

Pâté: The classic French preparation of ground meat or vegetables, fat, and seasonings. It can be smooth and spreadable or have a coarse texture, depending on if the meat is finely ground or chunky.

Peppercorn: A spice used to enhance the flavor of both sweet and savory foods that has three basic types: black, green, and white. It is most flavorful when used whole, but it also comes cracked, coarsely ground, and finely ground.

Pesto: Traditionally, an uncooked sauce of basil, garlic, pine nuts, Parmesan cheese, and olive oil, usually pureed in a food processor or crushed with a mortar and pestle.

Pilaf: A classic rice dish that is made by browning the rice before cooking it in stock. It can be prepared in various ways, such as with meats, vegetables, seafood, or seasonings like curry.

Poach: To cook food like meats, vegetables, fruits, and seafood in a liquid that is right below the boiling temperature. This enables the flavor of the liquid to infuse itself in the food being poached, as well as give it a tender texture at the end of the cooking process.

Poblano chili: This dark green pepper with a rich flavor, ranging from mild to hot in spiciness, is the chili most popularly used for chili relleno. The darker the chili, the richer the flavor. The ancho chili is the poblano chili in its dry form.

Polenta: An ingredient made from cornmeal that can be eaten either hot or cold. It can be cooked to both soft and firm form and is typically mixed with cheeses such as Gorgonzola or Parmesan for added flavor.

Puree: A food that has been mashed or cooked to a smooth, thick consistency. It is usually made out of fruits or vegetables and can be used to accompany a dish or thicken a sauce or soup. Food processors and blenders are most commonly used to puree foods.

Ragu: A meat sauce primarily served with pasta that is a staple of northern Italian cuisine. It consists of ground beef, tomatoes, onion, celery, carrots, white wine, and seasonings.

Ratatouille: A classic French dish that includes tomatoes, eggplant, bell peppers, zucchini, onion, garlic, and herbs cooked in olive oil that can be served hot or cold as a side dish or as the main dish. Traditionally, the vegetables are all cooked together, but they can also be cooked separately and combined at the end.

Red pepper flakes: A variety of hot red chili peppers that can also come as ground red pepper.

Reduce: To bring a liquid to a rapid boil and allow it to continue boiling until the volume of the liquid has reduced and the consistency has thickened. This concentrates the flavor of the liquid—which is usually stock, wine, or a sauce mixture—and gives it a more intense flavor.

Rémoulade: A classic French sauce served chilled with seafood and meats. It is a mayonnaise-based sauce combined with mustard, capers, chopped gherkins, anchovies, and herbs.

Render: To melt away the fat from meat by cooking it over low to medium heat so the fat becomes separated from the edible protein. Typically the fat is then drained from the meat and either discarded or used to cook another ingredient.

Risotto: An authentic Italian rice dish made with arborio rice, onions, white wine, and stock. It is an intense cooking technique and can be served with a multitude of ingredients, such as cheese, meat, mushrooms, vegetables, seafood, and herbs.

Roast: To cook food, such as tender meats and vegetables, uncovered in an oven. This is to create a moist interior combined with a dark exterior.

Rosemary: An herb from the mint family that has needlelike leaves and is highly aromatic and fragrant of lemon and pine. It can come fresh, dried, and in powder form and is ideal in seasoning foods with strong flavors, such as lamb and seafood.

Roulade: A classic French term describing a thin slice of meat that is rolled and filled with ingredients such as mushrooms, vegetables, cheese, or meat. It is typically browned on the stove before being baked or braised in a liquid such as wine.

Roux: Equal parts of flour and butter combined together and cooked over low heat and used as a base for sauces or a thickener for soups and stews. White, blond, and brown are three types of roux that depend on how long it is cooked and what type of fat is substituted for the butter.

Saffron: A yellowish-orange aromatic spice used to flavor and color foods that comes powdered and in threads. This spice is used in classic dishes, such as bouillabaisse, paella, and risotto, and is used in moderation because of its intense flavor.

Sage: A pungent herb that has a fuzzy grayish-green leaf with a slightly bitter taste that is almost similar to mint. It comes fresh, dried, and ground and is most common in meat, cheese, and some pasta dishes.

Sauté: To cook food quickly in a sauté pan over high heat with a small amount of fat (usually oil).

Scallion: Also known as a green onion. It has a white bulb base with a long, thin, green leafy end. Scallions can be used fresh whole with seafood, soups, or salads and can also be cooked in sauces or with meats.

Sear: To brown meat with a very hot heat source such as under a broiler, in a hot oven, or over high stove heat in order to brown the skin and lock in all the juices and moisture before further cooking takes place.

Serrano chili: A small chili that starts out green when it is young and turns red, then yellow, as it matures. It has a very hot, savory flavor and comes fresh, pickled, and canned in oil. This chili is mostly used in Mexican dishes, such as guacamole and salsa.

Sesame seed: A tiny flat seed that comes in shades of brown, black, red, and most popularly ivory. It has a nutty, almost sweet flavor and is used in both savory and sweet dishes.

Shallot: A member of the onion family, it looks similar to a garlic clove and comes in various shades of brown to rose. It has an onion flavor but tends to be sweeter and is most popularly used in sauces.

Simmer: To cook food in a liquid that has a temperature of 185°F—just hot enough that tiny bubbles begin to break the surface of the liquid.

Skim: To take the top layer of fat off of stocks, soups, and sauces or the frothy foam off of milk and cream.

Star anise: A star-shaped, dark brown spice that produces the anise seed. It has a slightly more bitter flavor than the anise seed, and it also comes ground. It is used in both sweet and savory dishes.

Steam: A cooking method that retains a food's flavor, shape, and texture. It consists of a steamer basket or a rack in a covered pot of water over medium to high heat.

Stock: A traditional mixture of meat or fish, vegetables, herbs, and seasonings that simmers for a certain amount of time and is then strained and used for soups, stews, and sauces. There are many different types of stocks, ranging from chicken and beef to vegetable and fish.

Sweat: A technique that requires cooking vegetables and/or herbs over low heat until aromatic. This allows the ingredients to cook in their own juices and the flavors to be released without browning or overcooking them.

Tapenade: A thick, pasty condiment traditionally made from olives, capers, anchovies, olive oil, lemon juice, and seasonings. It is usually served with fish, meat, or as a spread for bread.

Tarragon: A classic French herb with a narrow, dark green, pointed leaf that has a similar flavor to anise. It is used in traditional dishes, including chicken, fish, and vegetables, and in many sauces, such as béarnaise.

Thyme: This light lemon-mint–flavored herb is a member of the mint family and is bushy with tiny grayish-green leaves. It comes fresh, dried, and ground and is most commonly used to cook meats, vegetables, fish dishes, soups, and sauces.

Truffle: This round and odd-shaped fungus has a thick wrinkly skin and comes in two types: black and white. Truffles have a pungent perfumed fragrance and flavor and are ideal with sauces, pastas, risottos, omelets, cheese, and polentas. They come fresh, frozen, canned, in oil form, and in tube form.

Turmeric: This yellowish-orange spice is related to ginger and is the key ingredient in mustard and curry. It has a bitter, pungent flavor and comes fresh and dried.

Velouté sauce: A classic French sauce that uses chicken stock, veal stock, or fish fumet as its base and is thickened with white roux. It is often the base for other sauces and sometimes has eggs or creams added to it for further flavor and texture.

Vinaigrette: A basic oil and vinegar combination that is most commonly used as a salad dressing and as a sauce accompaniment for cold vegetable, meat, or fish dishes. It consists of three parts oil to one part vinegar and usually has a variety of other ingredients added to it for flavor enhancement.

Zest: The outermost skin of a citrus fruit, not including the inner white pith, which is typically removed with a zester or peeler. The oils of the zest are very fragrant and add much flavor to sweet and savory dishes as well as cooked and raw dishes.

Organizations

In an ideal world there would be plenty of time to create menus and recipes and to thoroughly test them. In truth your business will most likely require many more recipes than you will have time to develop or test. A good resource for thoroughly tested recipes is groups that represent various products, such as pork, almonds, and olive oil. These groups have the budgets to hire talented food writers, chefs, and stylists to develop and thoroughly test recipes, and they often have very user-friendly websites.

Almond Board of California
1150 9th Street, Suite 1500
Modesto, CA 95354-0845
www.almondsarein.com
This site has hundreds of recipes in multiple categories, all with nutritional breakdowns. This is also an excellent source of gluten-free recipes.

American Egg Board
1460 Renaissance Drive
Park Ridge, IL 60068
www.aeb.org
Hundreds of recipes in every category, including low carb, diet conscious, and budget-minded. Almost all recipes have photos.

American Lamb Board

7900 East Union Avenue, Suite 1003

Denver, CO 80237

www.americanlambboard.org

Large, searchable database of recipes, all of which have nutritional information. Recipes are searchable by keyword, category, cooking time, and cut of lamb.

California Milk Advisory Board

400 Oyster Point Boulevard, #220

San Francisco, CA 94080

www.realcaliforniacheese.com

Database of recipes searchable by type of cheese and course. Recipes have nutritional information provided. This site also has suggested cheese, wine, and fruit pairings.

California Table Grape Commission

392 West Fallbrook, Suite 101

Fresno, CA 93711

www.freshcaliforniagrapes.com

Searchable database of recipes. Search by keyword, category, or type of recipe (i.e., food service versus home). Modify search by specifying low-fat or quick recipes.

Cherry Marketing Institute

PO Box 30285

Lansing, MI 48909-7785

www.choosecherries.com

Recipes with photos in both consumer and food-service formats.

Louisiana Sweet Potato Commission

PO Box 2550

Baton Rouge, LA 70821-2550

www.sweetpotato.org

This site has recipes in several categories. All recipes include nutritional information.

National Cattleman's Beef Association

9110 East Nichols Avenue, Suite 300

Centennial, CO 80112

www.beef.org

www.beefitswhatsfordinner.com (for recipes)

Recipes organized by meal ideas, recipe type, cuts of beef, ethnic dishes, method, time, or eating light. Recipes have photos and nutritional information, as well as cook's tips.

National Honey Board

390 Lashley Street

Longmont, CO 80501-6054

www.honey.com

The National Honey Board site includes hundreds of recipes classified by category or searchable by keyword.

National Onion Association

4725 Crestridge Court

Loveland, CO 80537

www.onions-usa.org

The National Onion Association site includes some recipes and tips with nutritional information, and a few recipes with photos.

National Pork Board

PO Box 9114

Des Moines, IA 50306

www.otherwhitemeat.com

Thousands of recipes searchable by keyword, cooking time, and cuts of pork or browsable by category are featured on this site. Recipes include nutritional breakdown and photos, as well as serving suggestions, printable recipe cards, and video demonstrations.

Oso Sweet Onions

720 Second Avenue, #107

San Francisco, CA 94118

www.sweetonionsource.com

Recipes in several categories, even desserts, are on the Oso Sweet Onion site.

The Peanut Institute

403 North Henry Street

Alexandria, VA 22314

www.peanut-institute.org

Site features contest-winning recipes by category, as well as recipes from other sources.

Salmon of the Americas

194 Nassau Street

Princeton, NJ 08542

www.salmonoftheamericas.com

Many recipes, some from well-known chefs, are on this information-packed site. Included are links to additional websites with salmon recipes.

The Soyfoods Council

4554 NW 114th Street

Urbandale, IA 50322

www.thesoyfoodscouncil.com

This site has assorted recipes and tips in no particular order. Some recipes include nutritional information.

Sunkist Growers

14130 Riverside Drive

Sherman Oaks, CA 91381

www.sunkist.com

The Sunkist site has a recipe database searchable by course, type of citrus, cooking time, or keyword. Recipes can be instantly scaled up or down according to number of servings. Featured on this site are healthy recipes, many by featured chef Martin Yan, and lots of kid-friendly recipes.

TexaSweet Citrus Marketing Inc.

901 Business Park Drive, Suite 100

Mission, TX 78572

www.texasweet.com

Not many recipes, but the ones they do have are excellent.

U.S. Potato Board

7555 East Hamden, #412

Denver, CO 80231

www.uspotatoes.com

The U.S. Potato Board has a well-organized database searchable by category, main ingredient, cooking and prep time, or keyword.

USA Rice

4301 North Fairfax, Suite 425

Arlington, VA 22203

www.usarice.com

Award-winning recipes, a comprehensive search engine, and preparation and storage tips are all on this well-organized site.

Valley Fig Growers

5568 Gibraltar Drive

Pleasanton, CA 94588

www.valleyfig.com

Who knew there were so many ways to use dried figs? Recipes categorized by course.

Wisconsin Milk Marketing Board

8418 Excelsior Drive

Madison, WI 53717

www.wisdairy.com

A well-organized site, the Wisconsin Milk Marketing Board allows you to search its library of recipes by cheese variety, recipe category, or cooking method. There are also recipes for twenty-six different ethnic cuisines.

Other Sources

Many personal chefs cite other personal chefs as their best source of information and practical advice. Great information can also be found online, in books, and in magazines. Here are some oft-cited sources:

Magazines

Bon Appetit (www.epicurious.com/bonappetit) helps you to match certain herbs and spices with different foods so your client's taste buds are happy. They also have wonderful seasonal menus and recipes for your health-conscious clients.

Cooking Light (www.cookinglight.com) is a great magazine with a very informative website. Lots of healthy recipes and useful information on freezing all kinds of foods.

Cook's Illustrated (www.cooksillustrated.com) has fabulous tips and techniques that cut down on your cooking time so production goes faster. They also provide full menus for every holiday and season, as well as various cuisines from different countries.

Cuisine at Home (www.cuisinemag.com) gives fast and easy recipes and dishes that have restaurant-style results that your clients will be sure to love. They provide endless tips and techniques with these recipes by showing step-by-step photos.

Eating Well (www.eatingwell.com) provides current nutritional news on the most up-to-date and trendsetting diets and fads that your clients may be following. They give full nutritional analysis on single foods and ingredients that make up their recipes.

Vegetarian Times (www.vegetariantimes.com) includes all sorts of food substitutions for your client's protein-rich diet. They also give helpful facts on how your vegetarian client can have a well-balanced and healthy diet through many recipes.

Newsletters

Berkeley University Wellness Newsletter gives readers information on the latest diet news as well as facts on healthy and nutritious diet supplements and ingredient substitutions. If you subscribe, you can access their wellness handbook, which gives nutritional breakdowns and analysis on diets, diseases, and featured recipes. Subscribe by going to www.wellnessletter.com or by calling (800) 829-9170.

Center for the Advancement of Foodservice Educators Newsletter is the largest and most prestigious professional organization of chefs in the United States. They give member seminars, workshops, and national events to keep chefs abreast of all industry trends in cuisine. To subscribe or for more information, visit their website at www.acfchefs.org/subindex.html, or call (800) 624-9458.

Kitchen Cooks, the newsletter of the Culinary Institute of America (CIA), gives you access to many of the CIA's exclusive recipes and cookbooks for professional menus and cooking techniques. Learn the ins and outs of traditional and modern dishes, from seasonal menus to healthy menus. Go to www2.ciachef.edu/enews/subscribe.html, or call (800) 888-7850 for more information or to get a copy.

Tufts University Nutrition Newsletter and *Diabetic Newsletter* gives readers inside news on eating wisely and food safety tips. They include facts on nutrition for produce and other foods as well as the limitations and use of ingredients such as sugar and fat. You can find out more information on their website, www.tuft shealthletter.com, or call (352) 392-1778.

Online Resources

All Recipes: www.allrecipes.com
American Diabetes Association: www.diabetes.org
Chef 2 Chef: www.chef2chef.net
Cooking Light: www.cookinglight.com
Cook's Thesaurus: www.foodsubs.com
Epicurious: www.epicurious.com
Food and Nutrition Information Center: www.nal.usda.gov/fnic/
United States Personal Chef Association: www.uspca.com
WeightWatchers: www.weightwatchers.com

Appendix C: Useful Weights, Measures, and Guides

Per-Person Serving Quantities Chart

Meat and Poultry

Item	Quantity
Boneless beef, lamb, or pork	4–6 ounces
Bone-in steak or leg of lamb	6–8 ounces
Pork chops with bone	1 large
Pork or beef ribs or shanks	1 pound
Bone-in beef, pork, or lamb roasts	8–11 ounces
Boneless beef, pork, or lamb roasts	4–6 ounces
Bone-in chicken thighs, legs, or wings	2 pieces
Chicken breast	1 piece
Whole roast chicken or turkey	12 ounces
Whole roast duck or goose	2 pounds

Seafood

Type of seafood	Quantity
Crab meat, lobster meat, octopus, shrimp, scallops, squid	4–5 ounces
Whole fish, not cleaned (guts intact)	12–16 ounces
Cleaned fish (no guts)	8–12 ounces
Filets and steaks	5–8 ounces
Live lobster	1–2 pounds
Crab in shell	1–2 pounds
Mussels	12 each
Oysters and clams	4–6 each

Other Foods

Item	Quantity
Potatoes	3–4 ounces
Salad	3–4 ounces
Vegetables	3–4 ounces

Weights and Measures

Dry Goods

1 pound brown sugar = 3$\frac{1}{2}$ cups

2$\frac{1}{4}$ cups packed brown sugar = 1 pound

1 pound granulated sugar = 2$\frac{1}{4}$ cups

1 pound powdered sugar = 3$\frac{3}{4}$ cups

1 pound superfine sugar = 2$\frac{1}{4}$ cups

1 pound all-purpose flour = 3$\frac{3}{4}$ cups

1 pound whole wheat flour = 3$\frac{1}{3}$ cups

Meat and Poultry

3-pound chicken, cooked and shredded = 4 cups meat

1$\frac{1}{2}$ pounds chicken breasts, cooked and diced = 2 cups meat

1 pound crumbled cooked bacon = 3 cups

Pasta and Legumes

1 cup uncooked pasta = 2 cups cooked

7 ounces spaghetti = 4 cups cooked

1 cup uncooked macaroni = 2$\frac{2}{3}$ cups cooked

1 cup/7 ounces uncooked rice = 3 cups cooked

1 pound rice = 6 cups cooked

7 cups lentil puree = 1 pound dry lentils

6 cups split-pea puree = 1 pound split peas

2$\frac{1}{3}$ cups dry lentils or split peas = 1-pound bag

6 cups cooked beans = 1 pound dry beans (2$\frac{1}{2}$ cups)

Vegetables and Herbs

$\frac{1}{2}$ cup mashed potatoes = 1 medium potato

$1\frac{1}{2}$ cups cooked sweet potatoes = 1 pound fresh sweet potatoes

1 cup chopped onion = 1 large (5- to 6-ounce) onion

1 pound onions = 4 cups chopped

1 pound onions = 3 cups diced

1 pound (6–8 medium) carrots = 3 cups shredded carrots

5 cups cubed eggplant (14 ounces) = 1 medium eggplant

2 cups sliced fresh mushrooms = $\frac{1}{2}$ pound

3–4 cups shredded cabbage = $\frac{1}{2}$ small head cabbage

1 cup chopped bell pepper = 1 large bell pepper

1 cup diced celery = 2 medium ribs celery

$3\frac{1}{2}$ cups broccoli florets = 1 medium (9-ounce) bunch broccoli

2 tablespoons sliced green onion = 1 green onion

1 pound beets = 2 cups diced and cooked

1 pound pumpkin = 1 generous cup

1 pound fresh tomatoes = $1\frac{1}{2}$ cups peeled, seeded, and diced

1 pound zucchini = $3\frac{1}{2}$ cups sliced or 2 cups grated

1 pound raw spinach = 8 cups

1 pound cooked spinach = $1\frac{1}{2}$ cups

One 6-ounce bag of prewashed lettuce = approximately 3 cups

$\frac{1}{2}$ ounce fresh herbs = $\frac{1}{4}$ cup loose or 2 tablespoons chopped

Dairy

1 pound butter = 2 cups

3 ounces cream cheese = 6 tablespoons

1 cup grated Parmesan cheese = 3 ounces

1 cup egg whites = 8–10 eggs

1 cup egg yolks = 12–14 eggs

1 cup heavy cream = 2 cups whipped

1 pound grated cheese = $4\frac{1}{2}$ cups

Fruit

1 medium lemon = 2–4 teaspoons lemon juice and 1 teaspoon grated rind

1 medium orange = 4–5 tablespoons juice and 3–4 teaspoons grated rind

1 medium lime = 1½–2 teaspoons juice and ¾ teaspoon grated peel

1 pound cranberries = 3 cups sauce

1 quart berries = 3½ cups

1 pound cherries = 2½ cups pitted

1 medium (5- to 6-ounce) apple = 1 cup diced apples

1 pound apples (3 medium) = 1¼ cups applesauce

One 12-ounce bag cranberries = 2½ cups whole cranberries

3 medium bananas, mashed = 1 cup

Dried Fruit

1 pound raisins, seeded = 3 cups

1 pound dates, pitted = 2⅔ cups

1 pound dates, unpitted = 3½ cups

1½ cups candied fruit or peel = ½ pound

Miscellaneous

1 teaspoon dried herbs = 1 tablespoon fresh herbs

⅛ teaspoon garlic powder = 1 clove garlic

4 slices bread = 1 cup crumbs

80 tablespoons ground coffee = 1 pound

1 tablespoon Dijon mustard = 1 teaspoon dry mustard

Can Sizes

1-pound/16-ounce can = 1½ cups

2-pound/32-ounce can = 3 cups

2½-pound/40-ounce can = 3½ cups

3-pound/48-ounce can = 4 cups

10-pound/160-ounce can = 13 cups

Cooked Meat Temperature Guide*

For accuracy on finding the internal temperature of all cooked meats, use an instant-read thermometer (available at grocery and cookware stores).

Chicken
Thigh	165°–175°F
Breast	150°–160°F

Beef
Rare	120°–130°F
Medium-rare	130°–140°F
Medium	140°–150°F
Medium-well	150°–160°F

Lamb
Rare	125°F
Medium-rare	130°F
Medium	140°F
Ground lamb	140°F

Pork
All cuts	150°–160°F

Veal
Medium	145°–155°F
Medium-well	155°–160°F

*These internal temperatures yield what most cooks consider the optimum taste and texture, although some are lower than the 160°F suggested by the U.S. Food Safety and Inspection Service guidelines.

Seafood Substitution Chart

Sometimes it is difficult to find the fish or seafood suitable for certain dishes. This chart will help you choose appropriate substitutions.

Delicate-Textured Seafood

Mild flavored	Medium flavored	Strong flavored
Cod	Black cod	Bluefish
Crab	Butterfish	Mussels
Flounder	Perch (lake)	Oysters
Scallops	Whitefish	Sole

Medium-Textured Seafood

Mild flavored	Medium flavored	Strong flavored
Crawfish	Tuna (canned)	Salmon (canned)
Lobster	Mullet	Mackerel
Shrimp	Perch (ocean)	Smoked fish
Tilapia	Trout	
Orange roughy		

Strong-Textured Seafood

Mild flavored	Medium flavored	Strong flavored
Grouper	Catfish	Clams
Halibut	Mahi mahi	Salmon
Monkfish	Octopus	Swordfish
Sea bass	Pompano	Tuna
Snapper	Shark	
Squid		

Other Useful Measurements

pinch = approximately $1/8$ teaspoon

60 drops = 1 teaspoon

1 teaspoon = $1/16$ ounce or 5 milliliters

3 teaspoons = 1 tablespoon

1 tablespoon = $1/2$ ounce or 15 milliliters

16 tablespoons = 1 cup, $1/2$ pint, 8 ounces, or 237 milliliters

8 tablespoons = $1/2$ cup, 4 ounces, or 119 milliliters

4 tablespoons = $1/4$ cup, 2 ounces, or 59 milliliters

$5^1/3$ tablespoons = $1/3$ cup, $2^2/3$ ounces, or 79 milliliters

2 tablespoons = 1 ounce or $1/8$ cup

2 cups = 1 pint, 16 ounces, or 473 milliliters

4 cups = 1 quart, 32 ounces, 946 milliliters, or 1 liter

2 pints = 1 quart

$1^1/2$ fluid ounces = 1 jigger

4 quarts = 1 gallon, 128 ounces, 3,785 milliliters, or $3^3/4$ liters

Metric Conversion Tables

Ingredients and foods have the same weight but often are given in different measurements. To ensure that you make the correct conversions in portioning out your serving sizes for your clients, refer to the following chart.

Dry measurements

$1/16$ ounce	1 gram
$1/3$ ounce	10 grams
$1/2$ ounce	15 grams
1 ounce	28.35 grams (30 grams for cooking purposes)
$3^1/2$ ounces	100 grams
4 ounces ($1/4$ pound)	114 grams
5 ounces	140 grams
8 ounces ($1/2$ pound)	227 grams
9 ounces	250 grams or $1/4$ kilogram
16 ounces (1 pound)	453.6 grams (450 grams for cooking purposes)
18 ounces ($1^1/8$ pounds)	500 grams, or $1/2$ kilogram
32 ounces (2 pounds)	900 grams

36 ounces (2¼ pounds)	1,000 grams or 1 kilogram
3 pounds	1,350 grams or 1⅓ kilograms
4 pounds	2,800 grams or 1¾ kilograms

Liquid Measurements

1 teaspoon	5 milliliters
1 tablespoon	15 milliliters
1 fluid ounce (2 tablespoons)	30 milliliters
2 fluid ounces (¼ cup)	60 milliliters
8 fluid ounces (1 cup)	240 milliliters
16 fluid ounces (2 cups/1 pint)	480 milliliters
32 fluid ounces (2 pints/1 quart)	950 milliliters
128 fluid ounces (4 quarts/1 gallon)	3.75 liters

Temperature Table

Freezer	0°F
Refrigerator	8°–40°F
Cool room temperature	65°F
Warm room temperature	70°–75°F
Lukewarm or tepid liquid	95°F
Warm liquid	105°–115°F
Hot liquid	120°F
Boiling water	212°F
Rising bread	80°F
Low/slow oven	180°–200°F
Warm oven	300°–325°F
Moderate oven	350°–375°F
Hot oven	400°–450°F
Very hot oven	475°–500°F

Food Seasoning Guide

To help get the maximum flavor out of all your ingredients, here are some of the most perfect pairings of seasonings with foods that will make your clients' taste buds tingle.

Food	Seasoning
Beans, dried	Bay leaf, black pepper, cumin, garlic, parsley, thyme
Beans, green	Basil, black pepper, garlic, marjoram, savory, thyme
Beef	Bay leaf, black pepper, chili powder, cumin, garlic, ginger, thyme
Beets	Basil, dill, ginger, mint, mustard, parsley
Carrots	Cinnamon, dill, mint, nutmeg, parsley, savory, tarragon, thyme
Cauliflower	Chives, curry powder, nutmeg, parsley
Chicken	Basil, bay leaf, chives, cilantro, cinnamon, cloves, cumin, curry powder, garlic, ginger, marjoram, mustard, rosemary, sage, tarragon, thyme
Corn	Basil, chives, chili powder, dill, mint, parsley
Duck	Parsley, sage, thyme
Eggplant	Basil, cilantro, cumin, garlic, parsley, thyme
Fish	Basil, bay leaf, chervil, chives, cilantro, cumin, curry, dill, marjoram, mint, mustard, oregano, paprika, parsley, saffron, savory, tarragon, thyme
Lamb	Cumin, curry, garlic, mint, oregano, rosemary
Peas	Basil, marjoram, mint, parsley, savory, tarragon
Pork	Allspice, bay leaf, cumin, fennel, garlic, ginger, marjoram, mustard, rosemary, sage, thyme
Potatoes	Chives, dill, garlic, parsley, rosemary, thyme
Spinach	Curry, garlic, nutmeg
Squash, summer	Basil, chives, garlic, marjoram, oregano, parsley, savory
Squash, winter	Allspice, cinnamon, cloves, mace, nutmeg
Tomatoes	Basil, chives, garlic, marjoram, oregano, parsley, savory, tarragon, thyme
Turkey	Bay leaf, rosemary, sage, savory
Veal	Basil, bay leaf, lemon, parsley, savory, tarragon, thyme

Beef

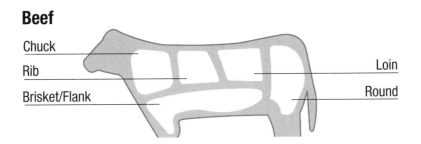

Chuck

Rib

Brisket/Flank

Loin

Round

Veal

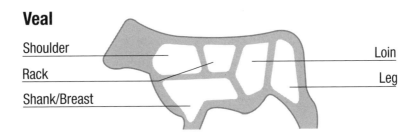

Shoulder

Rack

Shank/Breast

Loin

Leg

Pork

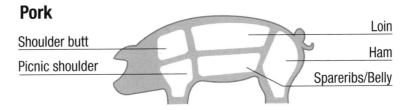

Shoulder butt

Picnic shoulder

Loin

Ham

Spareribs/Belly

Lamb

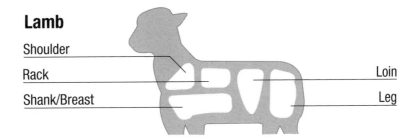

Shoulder

Rack

Shank/Breast

Loin

Leg

Standard Knife Cuts

Brunoise
1/8 x 1/8 x 1/8"

Small dice
1/4 x 1/4 x 1/4"

Medium dice
1/3 x 1/3 x 1/3"

Large dice
1/2 x 1/2 x 1/2"

Julienne
1/8 x 1/8 x 1"

Allumette
1/8 x 1/8 x 2"

Batonnet
1/4 x 1/4 x 2½"

Appendix D:
List of Personal Chefs
Interviewed

I'd like to thank all the personal chefs across the country who gave me their time and answered my many questions. These dedicated chefs shared their personal and professional experiences and have made this book more informative than it would have been without them!

John Bauhs
Resident Gourmet Personal Chef Service
www.residentgourmet.com

Constance (Connie) Breeden
It's Just a Matter of Thyme
www.justamatterofthyme.com

Carlin Breinig
Home Cooking Personal Chef Service
www.chefcarlin.com

Lisa Brisch
Dinner Thyme Personal Chef Service
www.dinner-thyme.com

Mike Cesario
Gourmet Express Personal Chef Service
www.gourmetexpresspcs.com

Randy Eckstein
chefrandy@charter.net

Hoyt and Lydia Eells
Your Kitchen Angels
eellsyka@aol.com

Wendy Gauthier
Chef Chic
www.chefchicaz.com

Sandy Hall
Dinners on Demand Personal Chef Service
www.dinnersondemand.biz

Margot LeRoy
Dinner Delight Personal Chef Service
chefmargot@comcast.net

Diane Lestina
Diane's in the Kitchen
www.chefdiane.com

Cathy Marella-Luce
Magical Meals
magicalmeals@mindspring.com

Marcie McCutchen
Chef for You Personal Chef Service and Catering
www.chef4u.net

John L. Mitchell
The Home Chef LLC, Personal Chef Service
www.mychefsite.com/thehomechef

Sara Myron
My Chef Sara
www.personalchefscooperative.com
(253) 225-4452

Elizabeth Ozaki
esozaki@sbcglobal.net

Linda Page
A Chef of Your Own
jpage1@adelphia.net

Brian Ramirez
Dining In Personal Chef Service
diningin@icwww.net

Pauline Reep
Pauline's Cuisine
www.paulinescuisine.com

Betsy Rogers
Ovens to Betsy!
www.ovenstobetsy.com

Linda Simon
Dine In Personal Chef Service
chef@dinein.us

Reid Smith
The Foodsmith Personal Chef Service
reidfoodsmith@aol.com

Mandy Unruh
Mandy's Meals
www.MandysMeals.com

Wendy Warman
Memorable Meals
wendy@memorable-meals.com

Scott Wilson
Healthy Home Cooking
http://www.k-t-p.net

Appendix E: Organizations for the Personal Chef

Personal chefs cite other personal chefs as the greatest source of practical and moral support and inspiration. As an example, there exists an e-mail group of about a dozen personal chefs that call themselves the Kitchen Bitches. They share recipes, ask each other for help, and generally inspire each other. Sandy Hall says, "We're from all parts of the country and have wildly different backgrounds, but we not only find one another hilarious, upstanding, and occasionally awe inspiring, we all bring something to the table when brainstorming is needed."

Local chapters of the United States Personal Chef Association, Women Chefs and Restaurateurs, International Association of Culinary Professionals, the Culinary Business Academy, and the American Culinary Federation are excellent groups that offer support and encouragement. Chef2chef.net also has an excellent personal chef forum.

The Small Business Administration (SBA) has many departments that can be of help to you. For free advice, contact someone from the Service Corps of Retired Executives (SCORE), or look up the services offered by the Women's Business Center. The SBA also has many small business development centers across the country to help you with business-related questions.

Your local chamber of commerce can provide you with all sorts of information to help grow your business.

Finding your own support system is crucial to your long-term success. Listed here are some of the places personal chefs across the country have found theirs.

Canadian Personal Chef Association

The Canadian Personal Chef Association (CPCA) was established during the summer of 1999 in response to a growing demand for training and support of this fledgling industry in Canada.

In their first four years, the CPCA trained more than 250 new personal chefs from coast to coast, using the industry's most widely recognized and respected training system developed by their partner organization: the United States Personal Chef Association. Since 2003 CPCA members have access to certification from the USPCA, a program endorsed by the U.S. government.

Members must complete a comprehensive training program, carry liability insurance, and operate according to a code of ethics. CPCA personal chefs must abide by health and safety regulations and must not cook in their own homes. Certified members upgrade their education on an annual basis in order to stay current.

The Canadian Personal Chef Association's mandate is to promote the personal chef industry as a quality and healthy in-home cooking service, and its members as leaders in their field.

Contact the Canadian Personal Chef Association at:
mia@personalchef.ca (please start your subject line with CPCA)
(416) 778-5870, ext. 3
www.pchef.ca

United States Personal Chef Association

The United States Personal Chefs Association is located in Rio Rancho, New Mexico. The organization has been thriving since 1991, with Gail Kenagy serving as CEO and President until late 2010 when she passed this duty onto Larry Lynch. Gail remains passionate and hands-on with thousands of personal chef members as she continues to work with the Culinary Business Academy, the USPCA personal chef training program. While professional chefs are welcome to join without further training, USPCA also provides complete training to those who wish to become personal chefs, and give them a great start towards a fulfilling and successful career!

The USPCA holds annual conferences, continuing education, and benefits of membership include liability insurance, Certified Personal Chef certification, Hireachef.com listing, MenuMagic software discount, Personal Chef magazine subscription, member only website, and local USPCA chapter membership.

For more information contact:

United States Personal Chef Association
4801 Lang Av, Suite 110
Albuquerque, NM 87109
Toll Free: 800-995-2138
www.uspca.com

Appendix F:
Business Resources

Books

These are the same books I recommend in my catering book. Why use them again?

Because these are the best business books I know. I've read them all, keep them on my bookshelves, and refer to them often when I have a problem or question I'm trying to solve. Look for used copies online. They create an excellent reference library.

- *7 Steps of Fearless Speaking*, Lilyan Wilder (Wiley, 1999)
- *101 Ways to Promote Yourself*, Raleigh Pinskey (Avon Books, 1999)
- *Book Yourself Solid*, Michael Port (Wiley, 2008)
- *The Consultant's Manual*, Thomas L. Greenbaum (Wiley, 1994)
- *Dig Your Well Before You're Thirsty*, Harvey Mackay (Doubleday, 1999)
- *Don't Sweat the Small Stuff*, Richard Carlson, Ph.D. (Little Brown, 1997)
- *Get Clients Now!*, C.J. Hayden (Amacom, 2007)
- *How to Start a Home-Based Business*, Bert Holtgy and Susan Shelly (Globe Pequot Press, 2009)
- *Secrets of the World's Top Sales Performers*, Christine Harvey (Bob Adams, Inc. Publishers, 1989, 1990)
- *The Seven Habits of Highly Effective People*, Stephen R. Covey (The Free Press, 2004)
- *Stephanie Winston's Best Organizing Tips: Quick, Simple Ways to Get Organized and Get On with Your Life*, Stephanie Winston (Fireside, 1996)
- *Success Is a Choice: Ten Steps to Overachieving in Business and Life*, Rick Pitino (Broadway Books, 1998)

- *Time Management for Dummies,* 2nd edition, Jeffery Mayer (Hungry Minds, Inc., 1999)
- *Time Management from the Inside Out,* 2nd edition, Julie Morgenstern (Simon & Schuster, 2004)
- *True Success,* Tom Morris, Ph.D. (Berkeley Press, 1995)
- *Zingerman's Guide to Giving Great Service,* Ari Weinzweig (Hyperion, 2004)

Software

Both of these companies have extensive product lists. Call and ask for additional information.

Business Resource Software
Plan Write
2013 Wells Branch Parkway, Suite 206
Austin, TX 78728
(800) 423-1228 or (512) 251-7541, Fax (512) 251-4401
www.brs-inc.com

Jian
Biz Plan Builder
104 Estates Drive
Chico, CA 95928
(800) 346–5426 or (530) 892–0233, Fax (530) 892–0233
www.jian.com

I ordered a thirty-five-page color brochure from Jian to see what this smart company was up to, and I was very impressed. They really know how to make the operations of your business easier! All it takes is filling in the blanks. They have thought of almost every software program, including business basics, an employee manual, marketing, publicity, a loan builder, and even a safety plan builder with specific information for food service.

Jian continuously updates this useful software. Get your hands on their brochure by calling the number or visiting the website. Your growing new personal chef business is almost guaranteed to have success!

Online Resources

The Small Business Classroom is an online resource of the Small Business Administration (www.sba.gov) for training and informing entrepreneurs and other students of enterprise. The classroom is designed to educate and provide interactive business guidance on a variety of topics to many types of students. Besides traditional small business clients, the online classroom benefits high school and college students, individuals with time and travel limitations, people with disabilities, and others.

At the classroom site you can read articles, take courses, or begin researching areas of small business development that interest you. Or, through a Service Corps of Retired Executives (SCORE) Cyber-Chapter, you can establish a confidential e-mail dialogue with an experienced business counselor. The following are some of the online classes that are available:

- Developing a Successful Business Plan
- How to Start a Small Business
- Managing and Growing Your Business
- Expanding Your Business
- Building Your Brand
- Advertising Your Brand
- Promoting Your Brand
- Building Your Website
- Assessing Financial Needs
- Tax and Accounting Basics

The United States Department of Agriculture (USDA) released a completely new food pyramid in 2005. It is not as graphically straightforward as the 1992 pyramid. The website (www.mypyramid.gov) features an interactive system that allows you to generate a standardized diet based on information provided on the user's age, sex, and physical activity.

The new pyramid is based on new and more accurate information about the relationship between newly discovered micronutrients and the prevention of life-expectancy–related diseases, like heart disease or cancer, as well as common diseases, like osteoporosis or diabetes. It provides much more detail about how much food to consume and offers your choice of twelve calorie plans, all balanced diets ranging from 1,600 to 2,000 calories per day, with about 300 free calories for individuals to consume without any guidance.

Using the new website you can now figure out the energy needs (calorically speaking) that individuals require based on a balanced diet focusing on fresh vegetables and fruits with the minimum of necessary fats. It takes into account vitamins contained in vegetables and fruits. It considers fibers and grains, which establish digestive regularity. It provides micronutrients, like calcium from its natural source, milk, which helps to prevent osteoporosis. The caloric and calcium needs are based on the intensity of physical activity and the age of the individual.

For example, I entered my age, sex, and amount of physical activity, and I instantly got this recommended diet:

Daily Food Intake:	1,600 total calories per day
Grains	5 ounces
Vegetables	2 cups
Fruits	1.5 cups
Milk	3 cups
Meat and beans	5 ounces
Oils	5 teaspoons
Extras (fats and sugars)	130 calories

The other information the website gave me was to aim for at least three whole grains a day. On a weekly basis, I am to eat 2 cups of dark green vegetables, 1.5 cups of orange vegetables, 2.5 cups dry beans and peas, 2.5 cups starchy vegetables, and 5.5 cups other vegetables. Anyway, you can put in information on your clients and get guidelines for what is considered by the USDA to be a healthy diet.

The site goes on to give you tips on all kinds of foods, what to eat as snacks, what to look for on food labels, and tips for children. There are also all kinds of tables and charts you can print out and refer to when figuring out your menus. You can print out the entire 80-page Dietary Guidelines report and worksheets for any daily calorie amount, as well as many other documents loaded with information. It's an information-rich site and very user-friendly.

Index

About the Author

Denise Vivaldo, whose Globe Pequot Press book *How to Start a Home-Based Catering Business* is in its sixth edition, worked as a personal chef while writing that book. In the cooking classes she teaches across the country, she meets students at every level and has seen a marked increase in interest in the personal chef field. She is also the author of *Do It For Less! Parties, Do It For Less! Weddings,* and *The Entertaining Encyclopedia. The Food Stylist's Handbook,* a book based on her decades of wide-ranging food-styling experience, was published in September of 2010, and *Perfect Table Settings: Easy and Elegant Ideas for Hundreds of Napkin Folds and Table Arrangements,* was published shortly thereafter. In addition to books, Denise is a contributing blogger for the Huffington Post as well as her own blog, Food Fanatics Unwashed. She lives in Los Angeles.